Quentin S. Crisp

THE PARIS NOTEBOOKS

Quentin S. Crisp was born in 1972, in North Devon, U.K. He studied Japanese at Durham University and graduated in 2000. He has had fiction published by Tartarus Press, PS Publishing, Eibonvale Press and others. He currently resides in Bexleyheath, and is editor for Chômu Press.

Quentin S. Crisp

THE PARIS NOTEBOOKS

THIS IS A SNUGGLY BOOK

ISBN: 978-1-943813-40-7

Contents

Volume I / 11
Volume II / 47
Volume III / 81

Author's Afterword / 123

THE PARIS NOTEBOOKS

Volume I

7th May

I suppose I don't feel bad.

As a writer I have had a vague interest in Paris for some time. I don't know exactly why. I suppose it's a romantic thing, although that sounds rather weak. Maybe it is slightly stronger to say it is a literary thing. Yes, I suppose that's it. I like French literature, and Paris seems like a literary place, and it seemed to me, therefore, a good idea to keep some kind of notebook while I'm here and see what happens, to draw inspiration from Paris, if there is any to be had, in the manner of my literary hero, Nagai Kafū.

I am writing this on the kitchen floor of a flat on the Rue Faidherbe, in the vicinity of the Bastille. I am very tired and I am alone. The flat is not mine; it belongs to S. In fact, it is because of her that I am here, since she sent me the Eurostar tickets as a birthday present.

I had never taken the Eurostar before. It was somewhat like catching a plane—the security procedure was similar. I was passing from one zone to another. The station, on the other side of the security barriers, where the various cafés and shops were, seemed very hot to me. I must have been sweating a little. It occurred to me as appropriate somehow that a centre for travel such as this should be so hot, when it is apparently travel that is responsible for the increasing heat of the planet.

I had a cup of Earl Grey while waiting to board, then, when the time came, made my way to the platform. When the train pulled away from the station and began the journey to France, one of my main impressions of the country I was leaving behind was the great number of CCTV cameras.

Eventually we entered a tunnel and after some time we emerged, and apparently we were in a different country. I was not sure this was true at first, until I saw a place name on a sign as we passed by. France looked very much like Britain in many ways, including the same dramatic grey clouds curling low overhead. However, I did begin to perceive—or in some cases possibly imagine—differences. For instance, I had the impression of greater space. There is no need here to hold one's breath and pack everything in quite so tightly. The foliage looked a little more scrubby and less wild. That is, it is a little less luxuriant, perhaps, and has more about it of cultivation, as if the landscape is a poodle rather than England's shaggy mongrel. The greens also seemed to be somewhat lighter in tone.

I feel my exhaustion catching up with me. Perhaps I should retire for the night and try again in the morning. I don't know what time S. will come round to meet me. Perhaps I will have some time after I awake to jot down a few more observations and record some more of the events of the day.

8th May

Morning (late)

Yesterday, S. bought flowers at what she claimed was the most beautiful florist in the world. She asked my advice, or perhaps merely my preference, on what flowers to buy.

"What for?" I asked. "For the room?"

"Yes, of course for the room."

She gave me a choice of peonies or lilacs.

"Well, in that case, naturally, I prefer peonies," I said.

"But I won't get these red ones," she said, indicating those we had just been looking at. "I'll get the pink ones." And she now indicated some whose buds had not yet opened.

When we got back to the flat she placed these in a glass vase on the table by the window.

When I woke up this morning I discovered that three of the buds had opened beautifully, their pale delicate pink blossoming to meet the milky daylight of Paris as it streams into S.'s gold-and-purple chamber through the gauzy gold veil across the window.

I have made myself an ad hoc breakfast of goat's cheese on bread, and fried tofu and mushrooms. While I was shaving with hand soap instead of shaving foam, the phone rang. It was S., suggesting we go to the cemetery. I suggested she bring her camera. "Of course," she said.

While I am here we are going to try and take a photograph for the dust jacket of *Shrike*. I have asked S. to work her powers to see if she can make me an icon. However, my neck at the moment is red raw from a rough shave. Maybe a scarf will cover it.

S. is, apparently, on her way here from her parents', so I suppose that this is not the time, either, to recount the events of my first day, lest I am interrupted at some vital point in the telling.

Perhaps I can give the barest skeleton of the day, however. Well, I arrived at the Gare du Nord on time, or possibly with minutes to spare. I was unsure what to do after stepping out on to the platform, but proceeded in what I presumed was the right direction, in which, after all, everyone else was proceeding. We came to a barrier that was not unlike the arrivals point of an airport, and there was S. with a golden-brown and orange twist of scarf in her hair, and a rather diaphanous dress. She greeted me with the continental kiss and informed me that her father was waiting in the car to take us to the flat.

Both S. and her father expressed their sorrow, and, as S. put it, their shame, at the results of the election. S. proceeded to tell me about how, immediately upon hearing of his victory, the new president had gone with various cronies from the press, along with the vilest of celebrities, to the most vulgarly expensive restaurant in Paris, to celebrate, and from there to a nightclub.

As we drove along the various streets I was given commentary. This is a lively street with people from many different cultures, on this street there is nothing but wholesale shops selling cheap Chinese fashion, quite to the detriment of the poor people in the neighbourhood, who have nowhere near to buy food. And so on.

Evening (late)

I don't know why, really, but I feel oppressed by a sense of doom at the moment. Maybe it's the heat in this top-floor flat, reminding me that all is vanity, and that our vanity is making a bonfire that will probably burn us all up with it. Or maybe it's because I got an e-mail from M. reminding me that D.'s seventieth birthday is on Thursday. Or maybe it's because I just read on the Internet some idiot saying he's read *Kinkakuji*, and that it 'sucked', and that the writer clearly had 'issues'. Who are these wankers?

Life, it seems, is constantly evaporating.

Anyway, yesterday S. showed me around her neighbourhood. We stopped for tea at her favourite café, where I had a cup of Keemun and some crumble (apple and pear, I believe), which served as my lunch. At some point we went into a shop selling Chinoiserie, and I ended up buying three postcard reproductions of old Chinese and Japanese posters. One shows a Chinese lady pushing her dainty little daughter on a bicycle. It seems to be advertising something, but I'm not sure what. There are pictures of cigarettes at the side. Could this really be advertising cigarettes? One shows a Japanese housewife, in sober-coloured kimono, with cigarettes in hand. These cigarettes are sold by the Westminster Tobacco Company Ltd. of

London, but they are Turkish AA cigarettes. The third postcard reproduces an image of uncertain origin. It appears to be of an actress, singer or similar starlet of the times, in monochrome. Her hair is shining and sculpted in finger-curls. She is holding her hands up to her shoulder and smiling coyly. The whole thing is rather soft-focus and dreamy. I am guessing by her looks, by the general feel of the picture, that the model is Chinese rather than Japanese. The girl also has something quaint and funny about her face. S. and I both laughed when we saw her, and that decided me in my choice of purchase. It seems S. and I share a taste for this kind of imagery.

At the same shop I also bought this notebook.

We visited other shops. I remember, in particular, a manga emporium — but I will leave their description for another time. Or perhaps I will never get round to it at all.

S. took me back to the flat. We came to the lift, and she invited me to "squeeze [my] body in", a line lifted from the documentary, *The Importance of Being Morrissey*. In fact, the lift was possibly the most cramped article of its kind I have ever known. It was really something of a squeeze for both of us to fit inside. I suggested that this really was a one-person lift, but S. pointed out that apparently it was designed (or intended) for three people.

I was very impressed by the décor of the flat. There is, of course, the maroon and gold wallpaper, and the gilt-framed pictures of Oscar Wilde, Louise Brookes, William Burroughs, Morrissey and so on. On the wall facing the bed the centrepiece is a pencil sketch of a naked male figure. This is none other than the Naked

Civil Servant himself, Quentin Crisp, drawn by an art student in one of the classes for which he was a life model.

I was given some explanation of the flat's facilities and so forth, since, the flat being very small, I was to spend the night alone here. In fact, I cooked my own dinner that night, improvising with tinned haricot beans, mushrooms, eggs, goat's cheese and bread. Since the light here is very dim, I found it easiest to write upon the kitchen floor (where the light is brighter).

Now I am writing at the desk, though the light from the desk lamp is somewhat inadequate.

And I suppose I must dispose of today, too, before I sleep, and so catch up. But perhaps I should not be so utilitarian about things. In any case, you never really can catch up.

I will say, however, before I turn in, that I had lunch with S.'s family, where I met her sister J. for the first time. After lunch, S., J. and I went to the famous cemetery whose name now escapes me. S. took some photographs of me. J. looked for—but did not find—Chopin's grave.

From there we visited what S. described, much to J.'s amusement, as "the Place of the Nation". And then we had drinks—Jasmine tea for S. and I, a blue lagoon for J.—at a nearby café, and finally came back to the flat for dinner, wine and Lieder.

At one point J. asked me who my favourite French writer is. Off the top of my head—since it was a difficult question—I named André Gide. She seemed pleased with this choice. She said, however, that no one reads him today. "Too precious. All that is history. No one reads him anymore. Only us."

9th May

(About 10.00 a.m.)

I suppose I really am rather precious. Occasionally I am reminded of this fact when I find how greatly my taste diverges from the norm. These days I find that I actually wish to discard a book I'm reading if it's not precious *enough*. In writing it seems people express a desire for matter-of-fact-ness in prose as if they are some oppressed minority overthrowing the tyrannical, vampiric aristocracy of ornate beauty. But they are not a minority. They are a loud, vulgar, bullying majority. That assumed straightforwardness is, to me, the most pretentious, and the most boring, artistic approach of all.

Action is boring. Events, for the most part, are boring. This becomes very clear indeed when one attempts to keep a diary of any sort. Jot down the events of the day, and really, as bare facts, who would ever care or find meaning in them? What matters in life, since the fact is, we never happen upon the big event we want, that somehow places us at the centre of the universe, what matters, then, in life, is texture, atmosphere and so on. This is really all that is left to us. We must enjoy ambience, or we must go to war out of boredom — one or the other. Personally, being precious, I prefer the former.

For some reason this reminds me of a couple of things that happened yesterday. The first of these was the response of S.'s father to a brooch I was wearing. It was a brooch of Napoleon, given to me by E.—a cheap little piece of kitsch. For S.'s father, however, it was like having an image of Hitler on my lapel. I had not previously given it much thought. It really had just been a brooch to me, little different to a Mickey Mouse badge or something similarly meaningless and tacky.

I think it was the revival of this subject later that day that precipitated a conversation about the relation of aesthetics and politics. We were in the café we went to after "the Place of the Nation" and J. said that she had never agreed with punks using swastikas as part of their fashion and imagery, and, moreover, that punk was uncreative and boring. I agreed to some extent, but added that I remembered punk, just about, when it actually happened in the seventies, and that, in the playground, it made perfect sense. Punk really was just kids. They didn't know or care what the swastika meant; all they knew was the adults didn't like it. I further added that fashion has often had dubious politics, if you want to read it politically. The original dandies, for instance, were English dressing in an aristocratic manner as a mark of defiance at the ideological austerity of the French Revolution. In other words, originally, to be a dandy was to be a royalist. Of course, the meaning has changed since then, and yet I cannot help feeling that something of the original meaning lingers. If I am something of a dandy (and perhaps I'm not) and if there are those who might conceivably sneer at my preciousness, perhaps it is because of some instinctive notion that I am trying to insinuate myself somehow into the ranks of the aristocracy, that I am, in short, a class traitor. Well, the former notion is false, but the latter is possibly true, since I hate class, all class, and have never felt myself to belong to any. I grew up amidst the working class, but for some reason, in my family, the working class signifiers were absent. The fact is, we had less money than most of the working class people around us, and even today I seem less likely to care about climbing social ladders or acquiring material wealth than most working class people. And yet, it is still quite likely that I might be perceived as a precious dandy, and sneered at for that fact. Why? Because I was academically bright, for one thing, and, perhaps most tellingly, because I care about beauty and despise all the brutish political movements that are an excuse for ugliness. So many seem to think that progress means dragging everyone down to the level of pigs to wallow in the filth of their own ignorance, and that the refusal to wallow in such filth is the mark of the traitor.

10ᵗʰ May

Yesterday S. phoned at about 11.00 a.m. to say that she would be somewhat later than she had anticipated, because she had got up late and still had quite a lot to do. For some reason I felt quite put out by this, even although I theoretically had things to do, too. I suppose I'm just not good at waiting, though I've done it all my life. Anyway, I was restless and decided to go outside on my own, visit a café, maybe do some writing there, buy some French cigarettes and be generally bohemian.

I had a café in mind, actually. It's very close and is called something like Le Café Pure. Apparently it was used in an episode of *ER*—so S. tells me. I left a note on the door to say where I had gone, but when I actually approached the café in question, I became daunted. It looked a little more like a pub than what I thought of as a café, and the bill of fare was not readily apparent. My French is almost non-existent and I had no confidence that this was the kind of place I could simply have a cup of tea (and perhaps a cigarette) whilst writing, so I beat a nervous retreat, and went in search of a more approachable, tea-drinking kind of café. As it happens, I did not actually find one. I stopped along the way at a bookshop—I believe it was gay and lesbian, but cannot be sure—and was flustered to be addressed by the lady behind the counter in French. I used what little French I had to explain that I was English and could not speak French. In somewhat condescending amusement—it seemed to me—she repeated herself in English. She was not unfriendly, but I felt increasingly nervous after that about going into shops and trying to speak French. At a corner somewhere I bought a small posy of lilies-of-the-valley, for which I am sure the woman charged me too much. I stuffed them in my outside breast pocket and decided to present them to S. later.

It occurred to me that 'objectively' (of course there's no such thing) life is always like this. We are always as lost and homeless as I was walking these strange streets, except we have varying amounts of cushioning against the ultimate homelessness of it all. In fact, I had some cushioning, too—the keys in my pocket, my bank cards, the phone numbers in my address book and so on.

Eventually I came back—without realising it, in fact—to the Rue Faidherbe, where the flat is located. I decided to walk in the opposite direction in the hope of finding an appropriate café, but none presented itself to me. Finally I went into some kind of sandwich bar of Indian provenance, with the name 'Ganesh' over the door. I ordered, in very broken French, a cheese panini, which I ate on the premises, like a tramp wolfing down a lucky find. I rehearsed in my head some phrase like, "*Avez vous le thé?*", but in the end could not bring myself to use it. I paid five euros, thinking to include the extra as a tip. The man gave me my change, and I was not sure what to do, but after some wavering replaced one euro on the counter.

Well, so much for being bohemian. No doubt, by this time, Nagai Kafū would have squandered half his money in the red-light district and known half the ladies there by name.

When S. arrived it was about 3.00 p.m. She seemed a little out of sorts, too. I gave her the lily-of-the-valley, which she put in water. We moved, in subdued fashion, towards the lift, the street, and the Metro.

Well, I suppose at some point during our visit to the Louvre we must have cheered up slightly, since it was a pleasant enough day, all told, despite my very sore, flat feet. I imagine we must have only seen a fraction of what is there to see at the Louvre. We started with Egyptian antiquities, moved to Greek and Roman statuary, and thence to Italian painting. I was surprised to find I quite liked the Graeco-Roman sculpture. At first, after the Egyptian exhibits, it all seemed tediously rational and Apollonian. After all, I reminded myself, it really is decadence and not classicism I admire in art. However, I had to admit a kind of muscular vibrancy to the statues that was strangely fleshly, despite the idealisation. There was also some very interesting subject matter, such as the torture of some unfortunate who lost a bet with—I believe— Apollo, and mischievous satyrs, and a hermaphrodite sprawled upon a bed. This last was a particular favourite of S.'s. I was moved to take photographs.

The mediaeval Italian paintings failed to move me. I rather think I hate mediaeval art—all those fluttering cherubs. Hang on, have I crossed over to the Renaissance now? Anyway, the Renaissance only seems slightly better—all these contrived religious allegories, before and after. I find it pious and insipid. What motivated these painters? How could anyone feel fulfilled painting this kind of thing? Stiff portraits, anaemic Christs—it's all another world whose values seem entirely inaccessible to me. Still, some of the colours are very vivid, and the composition is often impressive. It just seems chronically artificial to me, or, as S. expressed it, "kitsch". It certainly is kitsch, though I'm sure only retrospectively. I doubt that was the intention. To be honest, I don't even like Botticelli. When European art of that era was not tiresomely mannered it seems that it was so twee as to be negligible, however sublime the execution. But perhaps my tastes are rather strange. It's hard for me to tell. When we had the café conversation the other day about punk, nazis and so on, I also mentioned the fact that I have never felt that I really understand European classical music, or, in the same way, European painting.

Traditional Chinese and Japanese music, as well as traditional visual arts from those two countries, seems much more accessible to me. J. responded to this by saying that classical music is very complex and takes a long time to assimilate. I wonder if that's the only factor at work, though. There must be something about temperament, too, I would imagine. I wonder if I don't just hate the European tradition a little bit (in all the arts), with its emphasis on the human figure and society, on cold, hard mathematical ideals. I remember reading in Kafū's essay on the arts of Edo, how Western instruments were not suitable to Japanese music, and how Western media—marble sculpture, oil paints—were not suitable to the expression of the Japanese spirit. Western music he found mathematical and hard—like the sculpture. Traditional Japanese music he described as an imitation of the plaintive, threadbare music of nature—the chirping of insects, the cries of birds, the falling of leaves.

Anyway, soon we came to the paintings of da Vinci. "You can tell by the faces," said S. They were certainly better than what we had been looking at until then—the kitsch saints and angels with their golden tinsel halos—but I still felt that something was eluding me. Why did he paint these pictures? What did he find so fascinating in simple human figures? How did this fulfil his need for expression? It occurred to me, not for the first time, that my tastes and temperaments really are quite peripheral. It's little wonder that I appreciate the likes of Lovecraft. Really, what's so interesting about human beings that you would want to spend all your time painting them? It made me feel as if my emotions and sensibilities are somehow crippled looking at these paintings, and not really understanding when S. said that one of them—a rather dark painting of a figure pointing upwards—was powerful. Then again, if I am crippled I'm not the only one, and it seems entire cultures have leaned in the direction of this deficiency. Chinese landscape painting is testament to this. I recall particularly that Natsume Sōseki also discusses this—Sōseki who felt cheated by English literature—in *Kusamakura*.

Needless to say, we also saw the *Mona Lisa*. S. informed me that it was not too crowded that day, though there was still a substantial group of people straining to see the famous painting. We were able to get quite close—right next to the barrier, in fact. I looked at it for some time, a little irritated by the reflections on the protective glass.

"Do you think it's overrated?" asked S.

"Well, it has to be," I said. "It can only be overrated."

I wondered why it was this painting in particular that had somehow been chosen to be the most famous painting in the world.

"Well, there is something about it," said S.

"It is very pretty," I agreed.

"Not just that. It's the expression. An expression like that can only happen once, even with a real human being. But to capture that in painting, that very mysterious expression . . . "

It was true that the expression seemed alive in a way that none of the other human expressions in the paintings around us did. The *Mona Lisa* did seem to be looking back out of the canvas. And that expression, I suppose, is what has earned the painting its fame. But it's such a delicate, ineffable thing, that seems on the verge of disappearing altogether. And what, exactly, does it mean? I really could not fathom it.

"I wish I could see it without preconceptions," I said, "without knowing it's the *Mona Lisa*. But that's impossible, of course."

"Strangely, I do feel like I am seeing something new about it today."

"So, the most famous painting in the world!" I said, after some time.

It occurred to me that there is no better place to hide something than in the direct public gaze. The *Mona Lisa* is hidden in its exposure, and the greatest fame, somewhere, seamlessly, becomes the greatest obscurity.

So much for the *Mona Lisa*.

We next moved to another part of the building, which housed something that is apparently a particular fascination of S.'s. It was an exhibit that I believe was billed as 'funerary art'. What this consisted of was relics from mainly Roman tombs, from a period, S. told me, when Roman culture was influenced by Egyptian culture. S. was especially interested in the death masks—the facsimiles of the human faces and heads that were painted on the coffins, or sometimes were made in such a way that the occupants seemed to be raising their heads, looking up out of the coffins.

"This is beautifully done, do you see?" said S., indicating the painting on one of the coffins, "As if to say, look, this is the person here."

It did look as if the coffin lid had been half pulled away to reveal what was inside.

For some reason, however, the image that most sticks in my mind from this exhibition is that of the mummified head, little more than a skull covered in decaying blackness, but with the upper face anointed with gold. Apparently it was the Roman custom to apply gold directly to the faces of the dead in this way.

S. had explained her interest when we first came to the exhibition:

"You see, death is a serious business, and these people thought about it in a serious way and did what they could to respond. And this is it. They really wanted immortality, of course, and in a way they succeeded, because, well, here they are, still with us, thousands of years later."

And what best represented the human striving for immortality to me? A blackened, rotting human head, its face splashed with gold.

I thought of the lines from 'Quicksand', by Bowie:

I'm not a prophet or a Stone Age man,
Just a mortal with potential of a Superman.

I was very young when I first heard those lines and they were very powerful to me. They made me feel the weight of potential in my life—the terrible weight. And yet, at that age, I think I had the spirit to rise to the challenge. It's been a long time since I have thought about those lines and felt that way. Looking at the blackened skull I felt myself to be a failure, utterly lost. They had struggled far more heroically than I, it seemed, and this was what was left of them.

11th May

I can't remember now whether she was quoting Oscar
Wilde or Jeremy Reed, or quoting Jeremy Reed quoting
Oscar Wilde, but when we were at a café in the Louvre,
S. quoted someone to the effect that your deepest fears
always come true. She said that she hoped hers did
not come true; I said mine already had. Of course, she
asked me to explain.

"Well, I've failed at what I wanted to do, and I've
ended up alone."

"But there's still time," she said. "You're not about
to die right now."

And yet, I do feel as if there is no hope for me.

For some reason I had further intimations of this
hopelessness after looking at the paintings in the
Louvre and, yesterday, looking at more paintings, this
time an exhibition of Sargent and Sorolla. I'm terrible
with names, it seems, and all other such circumstantial
specifics necessary to 'realistic' fiction, but I do believe
that we saw this exhibition at Le Musée du Petit Palais.
No doubt I've written that incorrectly. Anyway, we
stopped at a kiosk where S. bought some postcards of
Parisian ladies in various states of undress. I suppose
they're courtesans or something like that. My *Time Out*
guide tells me that "[p]rostitution has always done
wonders for Parisian tourism", and that for centuries
Paris was "the Bangkok of Europe". How the glories
of this world fade! Left with a few monochrome postcards. S. asked me to choose one for myself, so I chose

one of a lady reclining on a couch, covering her mouth with her hand in a coy manner. She is wearing loose, white underwear, stockings, and a feather headdress. S. told me of some writer—Diderot apparently—who preferred symbolic eroticism to graphic eroticism. For instance, we saw one such picture that had caught his fancy, of a young girl holding a cracked jug. The girl herself was an ordinary-looking girl, fully clothed, but the cracked jug, it seemed, symbolised that she had lost her virginity. It's an interesting idea that such a symbol can be erotic. After all, it seems to me, for humans sex is all about symbolism, anyway. What else is a pair of stockings? What else red lips? What else the various words needed when you want to talk dirty? Looked at that way, why not a cracked jug?

Anyway, so, we had trouble finding the museum, until S. asked a policeman.

"I've just spoken to a cop," she said. "I'll have to go home and lie down for the rest of the day."

I took some photographs of S. and J. on the steps outside, and then we entered.

The exhibition was billed as something like, "Sargent and Sorolla—Painters of Light", and focused, unsurprisingly, on their treatment of light. The works were more or less alternated, so that there would be a space with Sorolla and then a space with Sargent and then with Sorolla again, and so on. At first I thought I could tell their styles apart quite well, but as we progressed along the designated route, I found them harder and harder to distinguish. I don't know if that was the idea.

I certainly enjoyed their work more than those etiolated Italian paintings, it has to be said. The thought even occurred to me, maybe this is what I mean by ambience. Maybe what I want to do with writing is what painters have been doing for a century and longer—catching a certain twist in someone's smile, a certain gleam in the eye, a certain attitude of the body, a certain effect of the light, in other words, a living moment. Some of the paintings felt like an eternal now. The summer Sorolla apparently spent painting at the beach was still now, and suffered from no distancing patina. *There* were the cooling winds off the sea, and *there* was the feel of the sunlight. I liked less, however, the paintings that seemed to be of rich families who had paid the painters to flatter them. There seemed to be no end of drawing rooms in the paintings. God help me, I'm a punk and a prole, after all, and must renounce my tentatively worn dandy credentials, but I began to hate all this polite art, whatever secret mischief the painters might have included, or whatever sweeping genius they might have employed in bringing the canvas to chromatic life. Why choose these moments to put in the genie's bottle of the eternal now? Why these people? It seems that they reek of the same flattery of rich patrons as classical music also does to me. And yet, I'm prepared to be mistaken on this point. I'm prepared to learn from someone else's genius to see things in a different way, and to put aside such grimy political considerations. I'm sure Sargent and Sorolla were really quite radical, anyway. For instance, there was a painting by Sorolla of young women huddled in a train carriage, about to be sold into the sex trade.

I suppose the thing that really bothered me was the same sense—though perhaps weaker—that I'd had at the Louvre, that something was eluding me. And once again it seemed to me that what I truly could not relate to was this focus on human figures, and that, naturally enough, the human figure is central to normal human feelings, but not, somehow, for me. And this is why I am crippled, and why my deepest fears have come true. I am on the periphery, away from the human centre of fame, prosperity, procreation and so on. It even feels to me that I have reached some kind of tipping point, and that there is no turning back. Heterosexuality — which once was convincingly presented to me by the world as obvious — I feel I understand less and less. In fact, I don't really think I understand any sexuality. Not that I don't have a sexuality myself, but it seems somehow vestigial now, like a man's nipples, existing without any actual use. I feel like a hybrid. I am sterile, an evolutionary dead end, here to spend my days in some scrubland of exile and to leave no mark upon anything, but only to witness in the moments before oblivion how everything shuts me out.

When we got back to the flat from the museum, after we had also done a little shopping for food, S. said she was exhausted, and was going back to her parents' to have a bath and go to bed. I did not want her to go, but naturally I did not protest since, well, that would have been childish and pointless. When she did leave, I was overcome by a crushing, oceanic wave of loneliness. It's here again, I thought, this is the indescribable taste of my deepest fear. I feel it in my body, a kind of tender quivering. I believe only someone who has felt it will be able to understand. There are no words for it — never have been and never will be — though I try again and again to express it indirectly through story.

This is as far as my life gets, I thought, and what it always comes back to. It is unbearable. It is precisely this loneliness that has paralysed me and made me a failure all my life. It paralyses me now. I cannot move from this chair. I have travelled the world, but I have never been an explorer. I have merely flung myself desperately here and there in the hope of shaking off this loneliness. It prostrated me in a hotel room in Taiwan. In Kyoto it gave me panic attacks. And here it is again in Paris. Some have hacked their way through the jungles of the Amazon. Surely their bodies were radiantly free of the infection of loneliness. Had it been me I would have sat upon the ground and wept, merely to be there, to be anywhere in the great home-lessness of the world, where there is nothing in the end to find, no destiny waiting, no soul mate, nothing except this air and this silence.

I remembered that S. had pointed out to me a bottle of red wine she had left in the flat, should I need it. I decided that I needed it now. I wanted to go out and explore the streets of Paris on my own, but I was too afraid. I thought the wine might help. In particular, I thought cigarettes might help, but, since I have 'given up', I would not be able to smoke without also having a little drink, for two reasons. First, cigarettes are now often disgusting to me without the accompaniment of alcohol, and second, it would give me an excuse—I have still given up, I'm only smoking because I've had a drink. Anyway, I had a glass of wine and went out in search of a place to buy cigarettes and more drink. The first place I noticed actually had an accordion player in it, but I noticed behind the bar there were bottles, but no cigarettes. I could not bring myself to go inside.

I think I need a 'tabac', I thought to myself. I thought of L., lovely L. The last time I was in Paris, it was with L. That was in the days they still had francs rather than euros. I remember her saying something about having to go to a 'tabac' to buy papers and tobacco for the cigarettes she rolled for us both.

I looked for a tabac, but none seemed to be open. I went into a 'general store' and stuttered out some French, performed a ridiculous mime of smoking, only to discover that the man understood the word 'cigarette' anyway. "*A la Place*," he said. I walked and walked. "*La Place*", it turned out, was The Place of the Nation. All the tabacs were closed, it seemed, and nowhere else seemed to sell cigarettes. I did not ask again, and I was too afraid simply to go in anywhere and order a drink or something to eat and have a general look around, though I did step inside a couple of bars or cafés or whatever they are. I completed a circuit of The Place of the Nation without realising. Finally I gave up on the idea of cigarettes. I should be enjoying Paris, I thought, making the most of it. Are these streets beautiful? Romantic? Perhaps they are, or would be, if only I had someone to share them with. I have really never had anyone to share any such moments with. It occurred to me that cigarettes have probably been the only thing that have made me able to enjoy, to some degree, my aloneness.

I came back to the flat and drank some more wine and worked on my novel, *The Lovers*.

12ᵗʰ May

Morning again. I suppose neither S. nor I are particularly early risers, or quick to get ready in the mornings, but I seem to be slightly the earlier and the quicker. Anyway, the situation is such that I have got into the habit of writing in the mornings before S. phones and comes round, and when the light is better to write and read by, too. So, I am now sitting at S.'s desk, having filled up the teapot—a huge, ornate item, quite in keeping with the general décor—with boiling water to brew *"rose thé"*, which I will drink from a china cup with a pink peony design. And this too has become my habit here. These preparations made, I may now write:

Satisfaction, it seems, is often a rather flat sensation, like a full stomach, and last night I had both satisfaction and a literal full stomach. To be brief, since I rose particularly late this morning, I finally entered and spent time in a café, all by myself. It was, in fact, Le Pure Café—the one I think I erroneously (typical for me) called Le Café Pure earlier. I have one of their cards before me now, so I know I'm right this time.

I suppose, for one thing, I had got a little bored of my own cooking, which has been, more or less uniformly, fried egg and mushrooms with bread and cheese, sometimes with fried tofu and cold tinned haricot beans. I think I had some instant miso soup once, too. Also, I was still bothered by my previous inability to enter a café on my own, and, on top of this, the events of that day—a quiet picnic in the park with S., she reading to me and I to her—had left me in good spirits, so that I was sufficiently buoyed, it seems, not to be deterred by large numbers of unknown people whose language I did not speak. Even so, I did not immediately find a café I could happily enter. I was not without trepidation. I was also looking for cigarettes, and the combined tabac and café that S. had—rather disapprovingly—pointed out for me earlier in the day was closed. Apart from the purchase of cigarettes, my main requirements were enough light to write by and no loud, annoying music. Well, after walking the length of the street—and the area is, as S. told me before I came, chock-full of cafés—I doubled back and settled on Le Pure Café. In other words, I had given up on cigarettes.

The café proved to be quite crowded, but by now my resolve was made, and after a couple left, I sat at the space they had vacated, by the bar. I managed to say something like "*Un vin rouge, s'il vous plait*" to the barman, and he gave me a drinks menu so that I could be a little more specific. I pointed at something on the menu, which was apparently not available, so I pointed to something else, which was. Next to me, some lantern-jawed American was talking to his companion about business, finance, various places he'd been to whose names he could not properly remember. He was sure that it was "Raspberry Hotel" or that the town was called something like "Glasberry". I noticed they were smoking. Naturally, I did not ask for a cigarette. Later I noticed them buy some cigarettes from the barman. So I *could* buy them here! In the end, for some reason, I didn't.

With my glass of red wine on the counter next to me, I took out my writing pad to do a little work on 'Sado-ga-shima'. The barman asked me if I was an "*ecrivain*", to which I replied in the affirmative. I also explained that I was English and could not speak French. He said something about himself being a writer, too, a little, and that he liked an American writer whose name I did not quite catch, but, if I understand correctly, was responsible for *L.A. Confidential*. I smiled indulgently, since language failed me.

Eventually, after I had successfully written just over a page, I had worked up enough courage to order food—I noticed others eating around me, so decided that food must be available here. I said something to the barman like, "*Je voudrais* [mime of looking at something] *la carte*." At first he pointed questioningly to what must have been the drinks menu. Then he asked me a question with the word "*mangez*" in it, and I nodded. He asked me if I would like to sit at a table. I nodded without actually understanding, or not at first, anyway. So, eventually I was whisked away to a little table that someone had just vacated, and was attended by a very thin, vivacious waitress who seemed to speak reasonable English.

After some negotiation, and my mention of the fact I am vegetarian, we arrived at an order of *salade du jour*, minus the sausage, or whatever the meat content had been. It was entirely sufficient to my appetite. I also had another glass of red wine.

So, this was my great triumph. Of course, it occurred to me what a trifling triumph it was, and, as mentioned, I felt a little flat on that account. There was the eternal question, "Is this it?" Was this to be, I wondered, the highlight of my existence, or one of them? It occurred to me, also, that I am something of a coward for not entering the pleasure quarters and claiming my triumph there as I had claimed it in this café. But, quite probably, the only reason I would wish to do so, anyway, would be to prove to myself that I am not a coward. And after I had sated myself there, what then? In all probability, I would feel the same flatness, and think again, "Is this it?" And if I were to follow that chain of enquiry indefinitely it would no doubt lead me to murder, and to war. And so I came back once more to the idea of ambience—of atmosphere—as the only antidote to this craving for some greater and greater event, some more dramatic happening. After all, if a cracked jug can be an erotic signifier, why can't wine and salad at a French café be to me a signifier of adventure? In France, Le Pure Café has become my cracked jug. Le Pure Café is to me pure no longer.

And as for the ambience of that place, yes, it was rather like a painting. Let us not be too eager to plot plots, but let us paint pictures. And this one, it seemed to me, was something like a Renoir. There was the central bar, surrounded by wooden tables and chairs, around which were the great sheets of glass that were the windowpanes. There were the rows of bottles in front of mirrors. There were the people, eating and drinking, lively but not rowdy, dressed, I thought, for the most part in a simple, elegant manner. The colour scheme was a pleasing combination of the black and dark blue of people's clothes with the seasoned, but fairly light brown of the furnishings. There was nothing of the dank, dark dismalness of the English pub, which becomes all too easily a place of Dickensian grotesquerie, or else simply a place of mean-spirited desolation, as might be expressed in some monologue by Alan Bennett. To a greenhorn like myself, everything in this café was pleasing. The people were closely packed, and seemed almost as if arranged for the convenience of the painter, and yet they were relaxed and breathed easily. People smoked unapologetically, but the atmosphere, it seemed to me, was not in the least a choking, unhealthy one. The staff were attentive and friendly. The food was filling and tasted good. People were drinking but not slouching into glass-eyed, nauseas disorder. And through the great glass window there was a dark street full of rain.

Later the same day, but past midnight, so technically the next day, I suppose . . .

My watch tells me it's now Sunday. I've just got back from dinner with S.'s family. It was the end to a very pleasant day, but I'm afraid that I have no time to write about it now, as I still want to write about yesterday, by which I mean Thursday. No, Friday. That's right. It's so hard to believe it's Saturday already. Or that is, it was. No, a writer can never, ever catch up with all that needs to be written. In fact, it's impossible for anyone to catch up with anything at all.

I just wanted to write a few words, however, about the picnic I had with S. on Friday (yesterday?), before I went out to Le Pure Café and after she took me to the shop of her friend J.—a kind of Chinese art shop, full of Chinoiserie, and with ornamental goldfish waddling about aquatically in tanks (Persian fish, as I called them).

Well, we prepared for the picnic by going to a cake shop, where S. purchased delicate-looking confections that were packed daintily in boxes for us. We had one each (I chose a raspberry and whipped cream thing). The park was one that S. had known since childhood. There we ate our cakes, drank the *"rose thé"* we had brought in a thermos flask, and, as previously mentioned, read to each other. S. read to me first. Her choice of story was Denton Welch's 'The Earth's Crust'. It put me in mind of some of the stories of Nagai Kafū. There was the same seemingly careless, but beautifully described accumulation of apparently incidental detail, and the ending which suddenly cast the whole in a different light. My choice of story was 'Hôrai' from Lafcadio Hearn's *Kwaidan*.

S. then showed me the garden adjoining the park, in which she used to play as a child. She remembered it as being more overgrown, and the pond then was more like a marsh, quite dangerous and deep, with stepping stones across which she would jump. I took some photographs of her there. The plants in that garden and her recounting her memories reminded me now more than ever of Kafū. I began to tell her how I had found the story she read me reminiscent of his work and attempted to outline some of his stories to give an idea of what I meant. I spoke about his story 'The Fox', which tells of the childhood memory of a fox that had its hole in the overgrown corner of the family's garden. We moved to another adjoining garden, where we took more photographs of each other next to the roses. As we were leaving, S. pointed out to me a patch of bamboo. She told me how the bamboo had once been so dense that it was hard to squeeze between the stalks. However, there had been problems because the homeless people had begun to use the place as a toilet, so those responsible for the gardens had had to thin the thicket out (into a thinet?). The ghost of Kafū was there before me in this little patch of bamboo. (In fact, in the foreword to *Dwarf Bamboo* he even explains that the title refers to his interest in things that should not be interesting as subject matter for a novel, the dwarf bamboo (*okamezasa*) that grows like weeds at the side of the path and on which people relieve themselves without a thought.) It occurred to me quietly but with sudden clarity that Kafū may well have saved my life. It's not that there is anything in his work that explicitly deals with the problem of suicide as in Camus' *The Myth of Sisyphus*. It's simply that knowing Kafū once existed, and that I have read his work, and can conjure his ghost up in a straggly patch of bamboo that was once used as a toilet by vagrants, somehow makes life seem good and worth living. Kafū, one of the least utilitarian of all writers, makes me realise that perhaps literature really is worthwhile, even if it sometimes seems egotistical and selfish. Is there in this some parallel with the Taoist idea of the usefulness of the useless?

We came back to the flat. Before I came to France, S. had asked me to choose some sample of Japanese literature to read to her in Japanese. I chose Nagai Kafū. In the flat, I read her '*Rōnga no Hotori*' ('By the Banks of the Rhône') from *Tales of France*. Kafū tells us how he has left America and his American lover behind him, and not long arrived in France, and now, every evening, lies down on the banks of the Rhône in the town of Lyon, just as twilight is thickening, and thinks of her. He concludes — though not unequivocally — that it is better to keep the beautiful dream of an unfulfilled love in his heart until his dying day, than to have the love fulfilled and let it become commonplace.

Well, I feel this entry in the notebook, too, is incomplete, but I must get up early tomorrow. I will lay down my pen for now, and sleep.

13th May

Well, S. should be here at eleven, and it's almost eleven now. What's more, there are only a few pages left in this notebook. I don't know what I'm going to write and I may not have space and time to write it.

I suppose it will be easiest for me to give a brief thumbnail sketch of the events of yesterday, to colour in later if necessary and possible. The plan had been that we would visit 'the Catacombs', whatever they are. I presume the name is self-explanatory. However, S. arrived here at about 3.00 p.m. and it was a little too late, since the catacombs apparently closed at 5.00. We decided to go, instead, to the bookshop, Shakespeare & Co. Also, we went to buy some film for S.'s camera so that we could complete our mission to take a fascinating photograph of me looking enigmatic and *noir* and, dare I say it, *shibui*, in Paris, for the back cover of *Shrike*.

The film was purchased at FNAC. We then had ice creams in cones—mango and passion fruit for me, fig for S.—looked in a second-hand clothes shop and entered the cathedral of Notre-Dame. I was duly impressed by the architecture, with its complex angles and orifices, like a Lovecraftian dream. We also took a great many photographs there, some of each other. We were there at the time of mass, and a sermon was being intoned while some fellow swung a censer. It was quite a feast of candlelight and incense. And then to Shakespeare & Co., which proved to be a very interesting bookshop indeed. I took some photos of S. outside, and she took some of me, and a rather beat (as in generation)-looking fellow with long white hair offered to take a photograph of both of us together.

"I don't do this often," he said, "but you two look benign."

He commented on S.'s clothes.

"What era is that? Thirties?"

"Yes. Well, twenties, actually. The Roaring Twenties."

He further remarked that our respective styles of dress seemed to match, and that we looked good together.

He took a couple of photographs of us from behind a small ornamental fountain, so that the jet of water appeared to be spurting up between us. Then S. took some photographs of him. From his conversation he appeared to be an American dividing his time between America and France (and possibly elsewhere). When I gave my name, he gave his as 'A.', pronounced in the

French fashion, with a silent 't'. Inside was a veritable citadel of books. I instantly had the sense that the shop had been and possibly still was the centre of a 'scene'. S. had suggested I try and do a reading there. I had not been overly keen on the idea when she suggested it, but now I knew that I wanted to.

While we were there, S. approached a very dandified character to ask if she could take his photograph. He happily gave his consent. He turned out to be from Norway, currently studying art in Italy.

I bought—rather extravagantly—three books. They were Baudelaire, *The Poems in Prose* (a bilingual edition), *The Moon and the Bonfires*, by Cesare Pavese (S.'s recommendation) and *From Blue to Black*, by Joel Lane. I had them stamped with the bookshop stamp.

Then we went to S.'s parents' home, where once more I was made to feel very welcome, and I wondered how I could possibly have deserved such favour, but now I have run out of space.

Volume II

13th May

(Continued)

It's Sunday. The petals of the peonies have begun to fall. They are scattered on the surface of the table now, and on the floor, as if the light itself were shedding its skin. Mixed with them is the confetti that S. showered on me earlier, wishing me a rather belated "Happy Birthday!"

She is gone now, back to her parents' home, and I have come out for an evening walk. I can well understand why Paris is the city of the *flaneur*. I walked the length of the Rue Charrone (no doubt I've got the name wrong) and doubled back, before entering this café (Le Peintre or something) and ordering a red wine. Now I am sitting at the counter and scribbling away. I leave on Tuesday. I think it was this morning that I filled up my other notebook. Although we went to the Sunday market, I didn't find a notebook there, and, after the market, S. and I spent the day in her flat. She cooked us a pizza, after which we had strawberries, and some kind of baklava-like pastries (maybe they even were baklava). S. said these were probably Turkish or . . . I forget the second place. They were not Moroccan, anyway. Moroccan pastry, she informed me, was the best in the world. The tea, however, was Moroccan-style—green tea with mint. After a while I supposed aloud that it was now too late for us to buy a notebook. It must have been about six by then. S. said it probably was (too late). However, she found this old notebook of hers for me. The pages are so small I may even fill this one, too, before I leave.

Earlier this week S. asked me if Paris looked like Paris. I said that I thought it did, perhaps in some places more than others. It was certainly different to London, I said. I found the area around the Louvre particularly Parisian. S. agreed. I have, in fact, been quite fascinated with the architecture since my arrival. Unfortunately I know nothing about architecture, so my power to analyse and describe just what it is that fascinates me, and how this differs from London, is very limited. Anyway, I find the streets here attractive and a pleasure to walk through. This evening, as I walked, it occurred to me that somehow, for some reason, and to some extent, a pressure had been lifted, and I no longer needed a cigarette or someone to share this experience with. At least, the pain of loneliness remained, but it did not quite prevent me from admitting that this *was* an experience, however evanescent, however solitary.

I even began to feel a kind of subtle intoxication, a kind of enchantment, as twilight slowly gave way to darkness. I stopped at a shop window full of differently coloured glass fashioned into ornate shapes. On the other side of the street, a strange celebration was taking place. In what appeared to be a shop emptied of furnishings and merchandise, brightly lit as if deliberately to emphasise its starkness, two little girls were laughing and chasing the balloons with which their adult playmates teased them. One young woman, dressed a little like a wedding guest, walked away from the game, as if for a rest, and lifted her dress to adjust her underwear, perhaps thinking that no one was looking. I walked on. In this light the pale façades of the buildings seemed to glow softly. Paris, it has occurred to me, is closer to the Mediterranean than England, not only geographically, but spiritually. The streets have something of the starkness that I imagine, and maybe even know to some extent, in the Mediterranean villa. The light surfaces seem made to reflect the sun, the straight lines, the elegant flatness of the rising walls in which the shuttered windows are set, made to increase the contrast between light and shadow. But there is also something here that is not Mediterranean, as if many autumns have softened these stark white façades with their bluer twilights and colder winds, so that the glow they return from the rays that bathe them has about it a hint of something melancholy, like moonlight.

Now I have finished my wine and will turn my steps homeward. Except, of course, that it is not my home. The street is full of cafés. I had to choose one. In the end, whatever I choose, it only seems to become my life. My dream remains in whatever I failed to choose.

14th May

S. collects images. I'm not sure exactly how to describe this fascination, but there's something about it that fascinates me in turn. I hesitate to call it fetishism, and not just because the psychiatric nuances of the word are too strong. It seems more like a kind of iconography, or an instinct to curate. I suppose it's not so different to what I do as a writer. In the words of David Bowie, in an early interview, describing his song-writing process, "I simply assemble points that interest me". The way S. treats images is, anyway, sufficiently different to my own obsessive curating as expressed in writing that it seems to me to throw a new light on the whole subject of obsession and curation. I feel that S. treats images like the pantheon of a personal mythology. So far, so much like myself. But she also seems to treat them as mementos of daydreams. Images become a cypher, each corresponding to personal memories and the feelings attached to them. A poem written in the language of these images, as with hieroglyphs, may have a meaning accessible to the general reader, but would also have an esoteric meaning inaccessible to any who did not possess the key to the encrypted code.

Her habit of collecting images is infectious. I believe I have picked it up while I have been here. I have not kept a strict record, but I am sure that on all of our excursions we have come back with images of some sort. I have even mentioned some of them. Often these images will be in the form of postcards or posters. If they are the right size S. will scan the images into her computer and add them to her vast and glittering archive. I suppose one way in which I was aware of this fascination of hers before coming here was through having instant-message conversations on the computer. S. would frequently change her avatar image throughout, as part of the conversation we were having. One moment it would be Louise Brookes, the next Morrissey, the next a picture of Charles Hawtrey or a damaged doll. The reservoir of images was bewildering and seemingly bottomless.

While we have been here I have purchased the Shanghai advertising images I mentioned. S. bought me the risqué monochrome postcard. At the Louvre I bought three postcards for myself, *Spring*, by Giuseppe Arcimboldo, a painting of a monkey in a studio, by Alexandre Gabriel Decamps, and *Saint Sebastian*, by Andrea Mantegna (I was looking for the one on which Mishima modelled the photo in which he took the role of Saint Sebastian—Guido Reni, I think). Later, when we were walking along by the Seine, looking for a cash machine so that I could buy something at Shakespeare and Co., I bought a print of what I suppose is the frontispiece of an old magazine called *Le Frou-Frou*. The picture, in Toulouse-Lautrec-style, shows a Parisian lady on a cushioned couch crossing one leg over the other in such a way that her underskirts, and possibly other underwear, are revealed in a great flurry of white, from which her legs emerge as if out of nowhere, stockinged in black. At the same place I bought a print in a similar style for S., the subject matter of which was cats. I believe that all the images

I have bought for myself (or S. has bought for me), S. has also scanned into her archive.

I don't think I can recount all the images that S. has bought while I've been here. Perhaps I will ask her for a list later. I am, however, sure that she purchased a postcard of *Madre* by Joaquin Sorolla, as well as postcards of a painting by Louis-Leopold Boilly showing a child with a cat, and a portrait of a lady by Jean-Baptiste Camille Corot. S. also tells me that recently she has been very much fascinated by old-style prints and paintings of roses and other flowers. She gave no reason for this when I asked her why, but, after all, why should there be a reason? Why not simply be fascinated?

Yesterday, S. put two more images on the wall, and I assisted a little, holding them in place. One of these images was of Proust, but one was an example of her new fascination. It was a poster she had bought at the Louvre, showing a veritable cornucopia of flowers, of all kinds, some in a vase, and some overflowing from some other, obscured, container. These flowers, along with grapes, pineapple and other fruit, are heaped in a kind of offering. It is not at first apparent, but the title of the painting leaves one in no doubt: All the sweetest efflorescence of life, its great fertility, is here laid on the barren stones of a tomb. As the title tells us, this is Julie's tomb. The painter is Jean-François Van Dael.

There is a kind of insect referred to in Japanese as '*minomushi*'. '*Mushi*' means (more or less) 'insect', and '*mino*' refers to the straw raincoat worn in Japan in days gone by. This insect gathers together bits of wood and stone—tiny detritus—and with these it makes itself a raincoat, its only home, into which it can disappear like a snail in a shell. This is a land insect. In Britain there is a water insect that has the same habit, but I don't know its name. I feel that what I do with stories and what S. does with images is not so very different to what this insect does. We find things, and we make a raincoat with them, to keep us warm, to protect us against storms. We build a home with them—separate things, that some might consider worthless bits and pieces, coming together to form a whole.

And why not stitch together a cloak for oneself that boasts images of Byron, Morrissey, Judy Garland, William Burroughs, Quentin Crisp, like the eyes on a peacock's tail?

I wonder to myself now if this is not a cloak of immortality. That is, anyway, how it appeals to me. And I have neglected to mention, amongst the images, the pictures I have been taking of S., and those she has been taking of me. Aren't these a part of the same iconography? I asked, after all, even if I said it humorously, whether S. could make an icon of me. Maybe this is more my preoccupation than S.'s, but I think that it will not be too difficult for S. to understand—S. who showed me the death masks of the Romans, who imitated the Egyptians in the search for immortality. Am I asking her to prepare my image for the tomb, my death mask? And here I was saying that I had no desire for social-climbing. Oh no, I am very humble indeed. All I want is immortality. But the thought of me as an immortal is frankly comic. And just when I think it's comical, and want to laugh—that's precisely when it seems possible.

Oh well, who cares in the end? Perhaps the closest anyone can ever get to immortality is to say "Who cares!" and mean it. I am torn between the desire for fame and the desire for obscurity. If the only immortality is to say "Who cares!", then obviously obscurity is closer to immortality. However, if I desire obscurity for that reason, isn't that a kind of fame I desire? And if I desire fame on the scale of the *Mona Lisa*, is that not simply because such fame will render me ultimately obscure?

About 7.30 p.m.

I don't know if I'll be able to write much at the moment. What I described previously—and inadequately—as a tender quivering, has returned. S. was meant to come round early in the afternoon, but apparently J. was ill, and she had to look after her. After some discussion with S. via text message and phone we arranged to meet later—around 6.00 or 6.30. I said I would go for a stroll in the meantime and be back by 6.00.

Later still—so late it's tomorrow

On my walk I began to feel something of the same enchantment I felt on my walk last night, even though twilight was still some time away. Really to describe the atmosphere that I feel in these streets would take some time, and time is something I do not now have. I have always synaesthetically associated autumn with a kind of light but melancholy blue colour, and have always associated that colour with France, probably through early reading in French literature, though I can't think now of a particular writer who has exactly the melancholy blue atmosphere I mean. Well, Tanizaki has it in *Sasameyuki*, definitely, but I mean French writers. Of course, Kafū also has it in *Tales of France*. Maybe Alain Fournier has it. Some of the impressionist painters have it, too. Baudelaire surely comes close, and maybe has it in places, but he's rather a special case. Anyway, it is exactly the atmosphere I would expect and desire from Paris. In fact, it is so much as it should be that I begin to wonder whether I am not projecting it. And yet, for the place to so consistently correspond to the subtlest nuances of that expected atmosphere suggests otherwise. My experience with Japan was different. I found a very different country to the one I had dreamt about. As I walked down the Paris street I thought to myself that I could happily live here. The city is like a pebble washed to smoothness by the melancholy blue tides of countless autumns. But I am to return home tomorrow, I thought, and this perfect soft blue mood will be lost again, the most fleeting and insubstantial of all dreams.

It started to rain, which only strengthened the taste of the blue. I ducked into a bookshop for shelter. It occurred to me to look for a French translation of Nagai Kafū as a present for S. To my surprise I found one—I think it was a translation of *Natsusugata*, which I have not read yet. What could be more perfectly light blue in mood than to duck into a bookshop out of the rain and find a French translation of Nagai Kafū? Unfortunately, I didn't have enough money to buy it. I will try and go back there tomorrow before I leave.

15th May

The day of departure. S. said something about coming around at 10.30. I wanted to get some presents for her, so went out early (just after 9.00), leaving a note on the door just in case. I discovered that the shops were not yet open. I came back to the flat to pack my things, judging that if I went out at 10.00 to get the presents, I should be back just in time. Again, I left a note on the door. It looked like I was going to be back in time. I was delayed by a few minutes, however, as the lady in the second shop wrapped my purchases. I think I got back to the flat at about 10.35. There was still no one here. The door was locked as I had left it, and the note was in place. Quite worried now, I entered the flat and phoned S.'s parents'. It wasn't that I expected her to be here at 10.30 so much as the worry that perhaps she had phoned during one of the two periods in which I was absent, and . . . well, thought I'd gone missing or something—I don't know. Anyway, the phone went straight on to the answering machine. I left a message, but I remember S. saying something last night about the phone not working properly. I then phoned the mobile phone—I'm not sure who it actually belongs to—and, after ringing for some time, that too went onto the answering machine. I left a message on that, too. Then I wrote S. an e-mail to explain what I had done. Then I tried both phones again, with the same result. It is now 11.20 and it seems I have no way of contacting S. and no way of knowing when she will arrive or if she will arrive or what is happening. Obviously my emotions at the moment are not entirely rational. There is something in this kind of situation that always makes me feel like a lost child. I feel incapable of doing anything at all until I know what is happening. It's as much as I can do at the moment to write this silly entry in my notebook in the hope of passing some of this dreadful dead time.

. . .

Well, I've just managed to get through to S. on the mobile phone. I asked if something was wrong, and she said, "Everything," at which my heart quailed inside me. I tried to explain how much this kind of situation affects me. I'm not sure she really understood, but she reassured me that whatever the everything was that was wrong, it was nothing to do with me, and that I had nothing to worry about on that score, and that she was ready and about to come in ten minutes or so.

I feel like I could cry.

18.12

Well, I am sitting on the Eurostar in Gare Du Nord station. Or should that be "at Gare Du Nord"? The train has just started to move even as I write. My sweat has just about cooled and dried and my heart just about slowed to a reasonable pace. I am hardly collected enough now to write about the events of this last day. It has, as S. said, been an emotional day. This emotional turbulence culminated with a rush through the rainy streets of Paris, and on the Metro, and finally, when the Metro train stopped at the station before Gare du Nord because of a problem on the track ahead, on the bus. I had that unbearable nervous feeling of the traveller that I would be late, would miss my embarkation, and be stranded. This nervousness is compounded by the fact that one does not really want to go, and yet, one is obliged by the situation to hurry and panic as if one cannot wait to go, and precious, difficult goodbyes are trampled underfoot in the rush like a rose dropped on the floor.

In fact, we did miss the train. I explained to one of the station staff that we had been delayed on the Metro and he kindly exchanged my ticket, giving me a seat on the next departure. I managed some sort of goodbye to S., but must have still been very flustered. When I went through the customs barrier, I realised I still had the keys to the flat.

I feel as if the plot, so to speak, of my time in Paris, has suddenly revealed itself on the last day to be as manifold as the petals of, well, of a blossoming peony. And yet, I am certainly not ready to write about such things yet, if I will ever be. I simply feel that something of significance has taken shape in the last week. As yet I do not understand it. I am an ignorant soul. I want to know the names of all the flowers, but sometimes my ignorance shows through. What I thought was a pink peony on my teacup may actually be a pink chrysanthemum. Or perhaps it is a peony, after all.

I found waiting for S. almost unbearable and the telephones were not working, and in the end I left the flat and walked in the direction from which S. would be coming. I had not walked far at all when I saw J. walking towards me. She explained because the phones were not working, and S. would be a little longer, she had come to see me and to give me a farewell card. I was very happy and relieved to see her. When I asked where S. was, she made a mime, which I suppose now was the application of mascara or eye-shadow, and said that she was doing her make-up.

We went back up to the flat together. She seemed to think she might be imposing on me, but I was very glad of the company. She gave me the card she had mentioned, and I gave her the Japanese versions of her name I had written. I had made two versions, each starting with the character 'kotobuki', which signifies luck and long life. One version terminated with the character for 'reason' or 'principle' and the other with the character for lapis lazuli. I asked if I might open my card now, and she told me that I must wait until I was on the train.

Eventually S. arrived with her mother. I went down to the foyer of the building to say goodbye to her mother, then returned to S., who had brought a big bag with all her things in, to move back into her flat. By now my childish impatience had evaporated and I was sorry I had ever been so selfish. I was glad to see her. Moreover, it was increasingly clear to me that a sad combination of factors had conspired against us at the end of my stay, and that there was nothing to be done about it.

Last night we went to the cinema. It was Anthony Hopkins' latest film. Entertaining enough, but I doubt I shall go out of my way to watch it again. We walked home together through the darkened Paris streets. It was my last night in Paris, and S. quite naturally wished to know how it had been for me. I said that I would be sad to leave. I suppose I must have also said something to the effect that my emotions whilst here had not always been of the lightest hue. She had been concerned at this, and when I asked why, replied, "Well, it's meant to be a holiday." My immediate and natural response was, "There's no such thing as a holiday." I added that wherever I went I was still me, and could not take a holiday from myself. I believe she understood. When, today, she expressed her regrets at the way things had been the last couple of days, I repeated my phrase of yesterday, "There's no such thing as a holiday."

Anyway, we still had time to take some photographs. We went to a café we had had our eye on as a location—a place with a kind of battered Rococo look—and, after ordering a couple of espressos, took some photographs there.

I suggested that we go somewhere else to have tea. While we were walking there, S. suddenly laughed at the idea of going from one café to another like this—not a pub crawl, but a café crawl. We had tea and cakes at the shop from which we had purchased our confections for the picnic. I had brought Okakura Tenshin's *The Book of Tea* with me, and thought it appropriate to read from it there. Halfway through the second page I began to choke up, and tears came to my eyes. I paused and started again.

But when we consider how small after all the cup of human enjoyment is, how soon overflowed with tears, how easily drained to the dregs in our quenchless thirst for infinity, we shall not blame ourselves for making so much of the tea-cup.

I read this far and my voice failed me. Tears rolled down my cheeks. I could read no more. S. lent me her dark glasses to hide my eyes.

"Do I look like a film star?" I asked.

16th *May*

S.'s flat is on the seventh floor. The usage here seems to be the same as the British. That is, the first floor is what the Americans would call the second floor. I'm not sure what the ground floor is called in French, but on the button in the lift were written the letters, "R/C". Anyway, that means the seventh-floor is the eighth storey. It is, as previously mentioned, the top floor. From the window one has a roofscape view of the Bastille area of Paris. In fact, the first photographs I took after arriving—actually I shall check . . . I have now checked. Some of the earliest photographs I took—on the morning of my second day in Paris— were of the roofscape view from the seventh floor window. I remember thinking at the time that they were rather commonplace photographs that would simply serve as a kind of factual memento for me. It was as if the idea of a roofscape itself was commonplace. On Monday the 14th of May, however, after I had gone for my stroll and got caught in the rain, I had occasion to wonder how I could ever have thought of such a thing as commonplace.

I came back to the flat, soaked from my walk, and sat down at the desk. I simply sat there. Through the window I could see the rain falling on the roofs of the city. Simply sitting here in this seventh floor flat, looking out at the rain-soaked city, is an experience of Paris, I thought to myself, it is a participation in one of the moods of the city. Suddenly my aerial position seemed extraordinary to me. This was another world, a Peter Pan world, seemingly separated from the terrestrial world by veils of mist. From somewhere the phrase "dreaming chimneypots" came back to me. That is exactly what I saw. Such a peculiar phrase— someone, somewhere obviously once had this same feeling, this same experience, to have arrived at it. I'm not even sure where it's from. It's even possible I've made it up, though I doubt it. It sounds like the kind of phrase Lovecraft might use in a story like 'The Strange High House in the Mist'. But it could just as easily be J. M. Barrie, I suppose. Or someone older.

On another occasion—but I can't remember whether it was before or after the dreaming chimneypots moment—I looked out of the window to see men working on the roof across the street. They were builders, and the roof was really quite like any other building site. It was flat and wide, and they walked confidently across it, pushing wheelbarrows full of cement and so on. The only difference was, this building site was in the sky. I thought of that moment in *Titus Groan* when Steerpike climbs into Fuschia's private chamber and tries to intrigue his way into her heart by speaking in a romantic, visionary fashion about the great field of stones in the sky that he has seen, with, if I remember correctly, somewhere a horse bathing amidst them. Or have I made the horse up, too?

In any case, at the time of the rain and the dreaming chimneypots, as time passed and the quivering tenderness—which is really a kind of dread at knowing that your worst fears will certainly come true and that the opposite of immortality will be your fate—was mixed in with my sense of calming wonder at the roofscape in which I had been lent this eyrie, I also remembered what S. had said about the music of Fauré and the way it makes her feel. Is this what she meant?

But now, anyway, I am back in Blighty, and all the notes I make on Paris and its moods must be made from memory. There is something a little unsatisfying about this, as if I am perpetrating a fraud. They say to experience the true cuisine of a country, you must go there, and, presumably, be there at the time of eating. And yet, I feel this notebook has not quite described its natural arc. There is still a little more to write.

I must confess here to a certain amount of artifice in the writing of this notebook. Not much, actually. Really not as much as might be expected. But some, nonetheless. I thought, before the time came, of what I considered a 'perfect ending' to the story. It was going to be our last day in Paris, and we were going to be in a hurry. I calculated that I would have some euros left over, but not enough for me to be able to change them into pounds back in Britain. So it would suddenly occur to me that a convenient way to get rid of my surplus currency was to purchase one or two Chinoiserie images from the shop near S.'s flat. Mementos of dreams.

What actually happened was that I offered to pay at the tea shop where I read from *The Book of Tea*, and where we realised we would miss the train if we did not hurry. I used up the last of my euros there. In fact, I didn't quite have enough to pay for everything, so S. gave me some change, too. We rushed back to the flat, took one or two last photographs there (in which I look bedraggled by rain), and bustled with my luggage into the tiny lift.

As we descended in the lift, it occurred to me how unsatisfactory it was not to have the rather poignant, suggestive ending with the Shanghai advertising images. I asked S. if we had time to make a small purchase. Since I now had no money, I would also have to ask her to make the purchase for me. Out in the rainy street, S. suggested she make the purchase for me later and send it on. Was there any postcard in particular that I wanted? I asked her to select one herself. She wanted to write to me anyway, she said, so she would send the card with her note.

Perhaps I can allow myself to keep writing in this notebook until the day that the card arrives.

17th May

I think it must have been when we were on our café-crawl, walking from the funky-Rococo joint to the tea-and-cakes place, just as we were passing the front door to the building containing S.'s flat, that I said something like, "It's sad, really, that human beings are so egotistical."

I really meant *sad*, too—not disgusting or infuriating.

"Well," said S., "what makes you say that all of a sudden?"

In fact, it seemed to me that what I said was the synthesis of a great many threads of my recent thought and experience, but I chose to home in on an immediate cause.

"Well, actually, this may sound strange, but I suppose it was because I saw the cover of the new Björk album in the window of the record shop we just passed."

"Really? What do you mean?"

"Well, you know, Björk doesn't really have the image of being egotistical, I think. Well, comparatively speaking. Compared to other pop stars."

"You think so? She's always seemed very self-obsessed to me."

"Well, yeah," I conceded with a chuckle. "Anyway, you know, it's like artists all seem to think that what they have to say is so important. There's Björk dressed up in this huge . . ." I gesticulated, ". . . this huge costume thing. And I'm exactly the same, you know. It's just sad."

A minute or two later, if I remember aright, I was directing S. to photograph me in front of a shop window displaying old manual typewriters.

I suppose I had been thinking in particular of the vast amount of the world's resources that go into sustaining the shy, whimsical, elfin creature known as Björk. Well then, I thought, is it better if human beings give up on all this extravagant self-expression and simply 'be', as their name suggests they should, as the rocks and plants do? Somehow the idea seemed untenable to me. To simply be, as the rocks are plants are, we would have to cease to be human, and be rocks and plants. We already have rocks and plants—no point in trying to emulate a different evolutionary phase, or rung-on-the-ladder, or . . . however you wish to express it. Any human problem demands a human solution. But is there a solution? Are human beings not intrinsically unbalanced and unbalancing? How unbearably sad and unfair it all seems.

I think it was on my last night in Paris, when we were walking back to the flat from the cinema, that we spoke about two things that somehow became connected in my mind. S. mentioned the violent storms that had been on the French news recently, which were, apparently, quite an aberration. "Like the earthquake in Kent recently," she said. "I would never have believed a few years ago that you could have an earthquake in England."

"Yes, yes. It's really very strange," I agreed.

I was gripped by a terrible fear and I did not dare say what I was thinking, that this was all part of the climate change overtaking the planet. All is vanity. All of this, every word and gesture, every fond memory, every idle dream and determined plan, will be torn to shreds and washed away, yea, unto the very words I write. None of us will get our immortality. No, no, no. Every human being will see their immortality swept away before their eyes with the rest of the wreckage, and not just every human being, but every root and leaf and flower, and not just every flower, but every rock and grain of sand, and not just every rock, but every atom of the air we breathe, and not just every atom, but you, God, you, who made it all I hope you're happy.

All our worst fears will certainly come true. That's the very nature of the beast.

Since I felt then, as we walked along, how utterly futile it was to think about the future, I wished for some way to make the present moment precious, to be—as a human being should be—with another human being. There came to me that ancient phrase 'carpe diem'. I have never liked the phrase, and I did not like it now. "Seize the day": that's how it's usually translated. But seize what? I have tried, and it has always, always slipped through my fingers. Once, under circumstances that I recall now as rather poignant, someone explained to me that a former boyfriend had told her that the actual phrase was closer in meaning to "Rape the day" or "Ravish the day". Why am I not surprised? Seize the day, rape the day—it's the same thing. It's a stupid, stupid Western idea. We have tried to seize and rape everything all throughout history, and the more we have seized, the more we have lost.

Nothing else came to me as to how I could make the moment precious, and I gave up hope.

The other thing we spoke about was the photographs. S. told me that—for technical reasons that I am not confident I can recount—her camera had been on the wrong setting for the film she had been using, and the photographs we had so far taken for the back cover of *Shrike* might come out a little grainy as a consequence. It was such a small thing indeed, this wrong setting on the camera, but she spoke about it with some regret. I, too, felt regret. And then—so be it. If we have no usable photographs, or if we have plenty, so be it. If this notebook is lost or torn to shreds or never read, or it if it published and (ha ha) lauded. So be it.

We are, anyway, helpless.

18ᵗʰ *May*

When we were in the Louvre, sitting down at one of those rather skeletal, airless cafés that you get inside such public buildings—like the cafés at train stations—S. asked me if I had ever tried to kill myself.

"Not very convincingly," I replied.

Well, after all, I'm still alive, and suicide is never very convincing unless successful. It seems as if it is only possible to take a person's suicide seriously when it is too late—a rather disgusting irony typical of human existence.

"The problem with suicide," I went on, "is that it's so very difficult to do, physically. And otherwise."

S. agreed:

"One thing I have never understood is why people can say it is the act of a coward. To take that step, I think, takes great courage."

I remembered fleetingly a conversation I had had many years ago. Someone, on learning I was a fan of The Smiths, had drawn a picture of Smiths fans with whom she was acquainted as sitting around discussing the ways in which they killed themselves last week. It was a fairly amusing memory.

This talk of suicide was part of a larger conversation about death, and what one is to do with this wretched existence until it arrives, willed or otherwise. It was a conversation appropriate to time and setting, since we had just finished viewing the exhibition of Roman and Egyptian funerary art, and I was feeling like an abject failure, as usual.

In answer to S.'s questions, or quite possibly without any prompting, I said that I had no idea what to do with my life. To be in such an adolescent state at the age of thirty-five is depressing, to say the least. Time and time again I have thrown myself into the world in the hope of finding life, and, specifically, my life, but all to no avail. There really does seem to be nothing—absolutely nothing—for me in this world. I envied, I said, those around me with careers, homes, life partners, but I knew that I was entirely incapable of sustaining such a lifestyle. When pressed, I managed to admit, "The only thing that comes close to giving my life purpose is writing. But that is something that's not recognised."

S. indicated that she understood, though I felt I had not really expressed myself adequately.

"I mean," I said, "there's this attitude that as a writer you deserve nothing, that you should be content with poverty and obscurity. But imagine if people took the same attitude towards, say, doctors: 'Well, being a doctor is what you want to do. It's a privilege, so you shouldn't expect any money or recognition from it. You should stack shelves during the day and practice medicine for nothing in the evenings.'"

It's no one's fault, exactly, except that if society at large had different values it would be easier for me to survive. In other words, an unfortunate difference of values between the majority of human beings and myself has rendered me 'a parasite' and not a very successful one, at that. They despise me (or would if they had heard of me); I despise them. There doesn't seem to be much of right or wrong about it. I did not ask to be born. That is my final defence. Can I help it if I'm not exactly what society ordered?

And so . . . and so . . . What are we to do with these, our useless lives? Sometimes I fear death; sometimes I desire it. S. told me that it's the same for everyone she knows, or at least, everyone she is close to. I'm not sure now whether she meant the fearing death, the desiring death, the regret at having been born, the sense of utter lostness and defeat in the face of existence—I think perhaps she meant all of it. Life is such a terrible, terrible thing.

It seems we're all of us alone, I thought. We're all alone, together. But I wondered, then, how that can be. What a strange, paradoxical thing it is. Let's not overthink this. I felt on the verge of turning inside-out, on the verge of touching something, of feeling, or understanding. If we're all alone together, shouldn't the all-ness and the together-ness of it cancel out the alone-ness? There's something here that I cannot quite describe. Please, please, let us not cling to small, resentful intellectualisations. Let us be expansive.

I subscribe to an e-mail group that sends a word of English vocabulary every day. At the bottom of each e-mail there is always a quote, unrelated to the selected vocabulary, chosen, I imagine, according to the whims of the editor. The e-mail for the 14th of May had the following quote, from Yasutani Roshi, apparently a Zen master:

> The fundamental delusion of humanity is to suppose that I am here and you are out there.

When I was having dinner with S.'s family—I suppose that was on the Friday, a week ago now, or was it the Saturday? Yes, the Saturday, I think—her parents asked me if I had made a wish at Notre-Dame. I had seen the mass of candles in the cathedral immediately as a photo opportunity and had lit at least one candle—possibly two—while posing for S.'s camera. Even at the time S. had told me to make a wish, but I hadn't bothered with that at all. I really had not given it a second thought. Why would I want to make a wish? My first and final thought on the matter. Thinking about it now, this seems to indicate that something really has changed in me. In the past I would always wish, quite fervently, on blown candles, shooting stars, dandelion seeds, magic numbers—anything of the kind. Now?

Well, apparently not. Somewhere deep inside the feeling has settled that it's really all the same whether one's wish comes true or not.

At the dinner table, after all this had gone through my mind in a fraction of a second, my reply was, "I have no wishes left."

Of course, there is ambiguity here. Earlier in the week, S. had played me a Lied (if I remember correctly the music was Schubert and the lyrics Goethe) in which the singer tells how he is looking forward to death, because he is utterly content with his life. I think that, at first, S.'s parents took my meaning to be something similar. Then, however, doubt crept in, and they wished to know what I meant. Did I mean that all my wishes had come true, or that I'd given up on having any of them come true? Was I content or despairing? Preferring ambiguity in most cases to the unequivocal, I made a tipping scales gesture with my right hand, one way and the other.

Obviously it was felt that I was hedging my bets and unwilling to announce my despair at the dinner table. S.'s mother turned to me and said something in French. I caught the word *"toujours"*. There seemed to be a strange certainty and strength in her words. They were translated for me.

"There is always hope."

And yet, I wonder if hope is not the problem itself. Perhaps there is only a very thin line between having no wishes out of contentment, and having no wishes out of despair.

And yet, again, I felt something of real value in the tone of those words before they were translated to me. Perhaps the problem is semantic. Perhaps what I really felt in those words was something like, "There's always a reason to go on living." Or, thinking now of the candle, perhaps I could translate that phrase in the words of Morrissey: "There is a light that never goes out."

19th May

Last night I met Drapeau outside his place of work, and we went back to Highgate Village for a drink. Our first stop was a rather unusual pub, named, I think, after some lord or other. There we both drank a couple of pints of TEA. Traditional English Ale, that is. We sat outside in a windy area that it seemed would be the smoking garden after the smoking ban takes effect in July.

"I haven't had a cigarette in three weeks," said Drap.

"Are you preparing for the ban?"

"Well, actually, I don't know how I'm going to cope when the ban comes in. I suppose we'll have to smoke outside on cold winter days."

I bought some overpriced crisps with the second round, after which we went on to the Gatehouse. We sat down at a table with a couple of pints of Black Adder and Drap said, "Actually, I could do with a cigarette. Do you want to go halves on a packet?"

I did. There was a machine right next to us, selling overpriced packets of sixteen cigarettes each. More expensive than normal packets and with fewer cigarettes, as if specifically designed for desperate people like us.

We moved to the smoking area, which had apparently shrunk, and stood there smoking until a nearby table was vacated. The ashtray began to fill, mainly on my account, and the pint glasses emptied.

On the way back to the flat, Drap purchased some food and pipe tobacco. I picked out some sandwiches. At the flat we had Red Bull and also red wine, but not mixed. We ate our viands and watched a couple of DVDs in a haze of alcohol and smoke.

The films we watched were both vintage seventies horror. There was *Deathline,* starring Donald Pleasance as a canny police inspector on the trail of a mentally deranged and disfigured cannibal who lurks in some disused section of the London Underground, and then there was *Dracula A.D. 1972* (incidentally the year of my birth), starring a young Stephanie Beacham as the dolly-bird grand-daughter of Professor Van Helsing, played by Peter Cushing. Miss Van Helsing gets mixed up in a graveyard rock 'n' roll black mass which summons Count Dracula from the grave to prey upon the hip young sybarites who have resurrected him. I remember the films through something of a fug. No, I think I mean 'fog'. The fuggy fog seemed rather appropriate to the films, however, as if that was exactly how they were meant to be viewed. It occurred to me that there was a very strong iconography in this flat, too, though of a somewhat different variety to that prevailing is S.'s. We slept. I woke up a couple of times before dawn to drink some water. In the morning, I looked, as is my wont, at the many books on the shelves. Thomas Ligotti. H. P. Lovecraft. Robert Aickman. M. R. James.

Arthur Machen. I seemed to see great tombstones rising up before me with the names carved into them, half worn away and obscured by lichen. We had coffee and croissants and watched another film. This one was a rather interesting hybrid. The title on the case was not the title in the opening credits. I only remember the latter now, which was *Let Sleeping Corpses Lie*. The film was a Spanish production in an English location. There was mention of Manchester and Southgate. The plot concerned a machine designed to eliminate pests in that area, by working on the nervous systems of insects to make them attack and kill each other. It had the unfortunate side effect of turning those recently deceased into flesh-eating undead. There was an ecological theme. This, too, was a seventies film. There was something about the filmography that gave it a continental air, strange in the Northern England backdrop.

"I suppose they wanted an exotic setting," I remarked.

Drap agreed that they probably did, although to us, of course, England is the very opposite of exotic. English place names, dropped into a story in the right way, have the bathetic quality fundamental to comedy. What is the title of that Eric Morecambe autobiography? *Not So Much Hollywood as Cricklewood*. Something like that.

Anyway, not for the first time, I had occasion to admire Drap's encyclopaedic knowledge of the horror genre, and his connoisseurship of the grainy, the neglected, the seedy.

Both of us had a bit of a hangover (I also noticed a copy of *Hangover Square* on the bookshelves and thought again what a great title it is), and Drap said, "Greasy spoon? Best thing for a hangover."

I was in complete agreement.

We walked to the greasy spoon café just up the road. Both of us ordered veggie full-English breakfasts, with tea.

"I like greasy spoon cafés," I said. "Aesthetically, I mean. This kind of thing." I indicated the grouped condiments with brown and tomato sauce, just before taking a photograph of them and the ashtray with a teabag in it.

I also took a few photographs of Drap, who was looking very dapper and *shibui* in his hound's tooth jacket. I sometimes wonder if I use the Japanese word '*shibui*' correctly. To me it is an expression of the greatest sense of taste and style in a monochrome, downbeat sort of way. My great touchstone for understanding *shibui* is Nagai Kafū. I think of the photograph of him in his hat and raincoat leaving one of his favourite haunts, Arizona Kitchen, or the photograph of him giving a broad, gap-toothed grin. I think of his restrained prose, like sunlight through a paper screen. *Shibui* is not the only style I admire. Mishima, for instance, liked colour, and gold, and all things that dazzle and glitter. He is almost the opposite of Kafū in this respect. Kafū is somehow sepia.

"It'll be a shame when you can't smoke in these places anymore," I said. "Greasy spoons should be, well, greasy. And grimy. And smoky."

I slurped at my tea. It was poorly brewed, but quite typical.

"There's a particular smell to builder's tea," I further remarked. "I haven't smelt it for a while."

I suppose all of this was leading me to ponder exactly what the greasy spoon aesthetic is, and I mentioned the photographer Martin Parr, whom I thought had captured it in some of his photographs.

"You know," I said, as if reaching a conclusion, "there's something that happens when you cross the Channel."

"What, to the Continent?"

"Or the other way."

"Yes. I know what you mean. I wonder what would happen if you tried to set up a traditional greasy spoon caff in Paris."

What exactly was this aesthetic that I saw in the tacky grouping of condiments here, as perfect as a red postbox? There is something altogether buttoned-down, altogether quaint and repressed, like a caricature of humanity.

Feeling revived after the meal, we stepped into Oxfam to peruse the second-hand books. I bought a copy of *The Well of Loneliness*, by Radclyffe Hall. The woman behind the counter was very friendly, and seemed to approve of my choice. "I've read it, many years ago. It's a little dated, but very interesting."

There was no price written on it, but she let me have it for one pound.

"Do you know she's buried in Highgate Cemetery?" said Drap, referring to Radclyffe Hall.

I said that I did.

We parted at Highgate Underground station.

I noticed there were no trains going towards Waterloo, but decided to change at Euston. There I discovered that the Charing Cross branch of the Northern Line was out of action all weekend. "Somebody really should pay for this," I thought. "Our trains are just not even funny anymore. Bring on the guillotine. When, tell me, when will we have a revolution and give these bastards what they deserve?"

During our drunken haze of the previous evening I had spoken to Drap about my stay in Paris and shown him some of the photographs on my camera.

"What, is S. an Anglophile?" he asked. This tendency was obviously visible.

"Yes. Very much so."

When I first learnt that S. was afflicted with the quaint malaise of Anglophilia, I found it difficult to understand. After visiting her in Paris, I believe I had a better idea of it, though not a very well-defined or articulate one.

She had explained her Anglophilia when I first asked in terms of an interest in the English eccentric, a figure that she had not found around her in France. "Of course, I learned later that there have been eccentrics in France, too, but when I first learnt about the English eccentric it was an *idée* that was very important and dear to me."

In France, it seemed to me, there was a living, natural stylishness in everyday existence. There was a more visible sense of breathing humanity. But that in itself can become an assumption, a paradigm of conformity. The crippling constraints of English repression and ugliness, however, occasionally produce the charming, crooked, strangely beautiful bonsai of the English eccentric.

Volume III

20th May

This cannot go on much longer. I am not in Paris and I did not even acquire this particular notebook in Paris. What's more, the last entry I wrote—the entry closing the second volume of this notebook—was mainly about England. With that, it seems, the death knell of this particular writing project has been sounded.

However, it is not over quite yet. I feel the will, like that of a dying man, to struggle on just a little further. There are things still to say. Maybe I will not be able to say all of them before I gasp my last. Maybe I will have to give up on my sad reflections about how, in order to talk to human beings at all, I had to become a fake, learning my lines from people wittier than I, and more erudite. Maybe I will not find the appropriate place to launch my attack on all that I hate in literature via a discussion of the greater availability of Japanese literature in French translation than in English translation. Ah, the brittle arrogance of the English-speaking world! The loathsomeness of the Protestant work ethic underlying Anglo-American literature, the twin, dominating influences of Christianity and science, both of them pushing the spirit away into some nether region of the inaccessible, both of them fostering a vile imperialism of thought.

Well, as I say, maybe I won't have the time and space for that one. To catch up, after all, is impossible. Death will come, and will discover that, in my allotted time, I have accomplished nothing but some inky, nonsensical scribbling, and that I *have not even begun* to answer the question set in this exam. To be fair, though, wouldn't it help if someone actually told us what the question was?

Anyway, Death, I have not finished yet, and since you have not the grace to tell us what the question is, you will excuse me if I scribble like an errant schoolboy. At least I can claim, as an excuse for prolonging things, that this third notebook is somehow appropriate to my purpose. It is a Moleskine notebook, which I was given by a friend on my birthday, and Moleskine notebooks, so the history tells me, were originally produced in France to supply the stationers of Paris. So, in a way, this is still legitimately a Paris notebook, even if this particular one was made in Italy.

The history also reminds me—and informs where I did not know—of the particular tradition to which I am heir in writing a notebook like this. To be honest, my conscious models are more Japanese. There are the *zuihitsu*—discursive essays that wander like a *flaneur* wherever the writer's fancy leads, thus '*zui*', 'follow', and '*hitsu*', 'brush', which equals 'following the brush'. There is also the extensive diary literature, though I must immediately disavow any but the most ambivalent allegiance to Sei Shōnagon's *The Pillow Book*. An interesting document in an interesting style, from an author chronically ravaged by the disease of snobbery and pathologically obsessed with trivialities. No, let us forget the insipid Sei Shōnagon, after all. My models are . . . well, need I even mention Kafū at this stage? Then there are also the likes of Kenkō Hōshi and Kamo no Chōmei. Bashō, too, I suppose, though he does not translate well, at all.

The history of the Moleskine gives my Western predecessors thus:

"Moleskine is the legendary notebook used by European artists and thinkers for the past two centuries, from Van Gogh to Picasso, from Ernest Hemingway to Bruce Chatwin."

Van Gogh, I like.

Hemingway? I have never had any desire to read Hemingway since learning of his predilection for killing animals as some kind of 'experience'. This is the very quintessence of the history of Western thought, it seems to me. How self-important, thinking that animals should die in order to satisfy his quest for some kind of macho profundity. I suppose that does not preclude the possibility he was a good writer, but I already feel as if I hate everything he stood for, and on top of that, I gather he had an aversion to 'fancy writing'. I imagine him using his typewriter keys as punchbags for his fat fingers, writing 'the great American novel' as if it's some kind of workout at the gym. A lot of the right people seem to like him, but I certainly feel no desire to belong to any tradition of which he is a part.

Picasso? Not really a fan. For some reason I don't much like the colour orange in paintings, as used to conjure up a particular kind of sun-drenched landscape with adobe walls and so on. I just cannot connect emotionally to that particular form of . . . I'm not sure what to call it. You see it a great deal in paintings claiming some kind of African influence. I don't really believe it. It all looks very coffee-bar to me, and not in a good way. Anyway, Picasso reminds me of that much of the time. There seems to be no hint of autumn in his soul.

Bruce Chatwin I knew nothing about until I looked him up on the Internet today. From the information about him on Wikipedia, he might just be the most interesting of all the four names mentioned, and it sounds as if what I'm doing with this notebook is closer in spirit to what he did than to any of the others.

It's funny I should end up polarising East and West like this when what I really want to write about now is the breaking down of divisions. There have been moments in my life, in fact, when, disillusioned with the respective shortcomings of both Eastern and Western culture (particularly in the realms of philosophy and religion) I have been overcome by the rather grandiose but inspiring notion that what I'm here for is to create some kind of useful synthesis of the two. Well, I said it was grandiose, but why not, after all? Western soul with Eastern subtlety. Western individualism with Eastern flow. In other words, I don't think either side really gives us the whole picture. Christianity seems incredibly prone to dogma and self-righteousness, but Buddhism has no place in its cosmology for passion and love. If only I could marry what is best in both of them.

After lunch

In my first notebook I concluded that A. was an American dividing his time between America and France. There were ample reasons for this. His accent and his manner were convincingly American, and, of course, he mentioned a home in America. The French pronunciation of his name could have been an affectation. However, when I spoke with S. about this later she revived my doubts on the subject, saying she had been unable to tell whether he were French or American. This, in fact, had been my initial impression. He addressed S. half the time in French, which, by her account, had been convincingly native. Perhaps the name A., pronounced with a silent 't', had been the final clue to his true origins.

I mentioned before that when I entered Shakespeare & Co. after A. had taken our photo, I at once had the impression it was now, or had once been, the centre of some kind of scene. Of course, I immediately felt excluded, and wondered what it would have been like to be part of the charmed circle of the great or fêted or hip writers. That's living, I thought to myself, though I was not precisely sure *what* was living. But since I was physically present in Shakespeare and Co. and still felt excluded, I began to wonder if I would ever feel myself to be living, to be where it's at and what's happening, even if I were acknowledged to be part of some charmed circle or other. Supposing literary history includes my name somewhere on the long list of writers who form the 'company' beneath Shakespeare, would I ever, actually, feel it? Or is the centre of the charmed circle always hollow? Maybe I even am part of a charmed circle without knowing it.

At times, alone in S.'s flat, I felt myself a visitor to a world in which I would never actually belong. I wondered what it would be like for this gold acanthus-leaf on its purple-red background, studded with gilt-framed but monochrome stars I have already named, to be my world. I suppose I will never know. This in itself is sad. But then I wondered if S. would ever know what her world looked like from the outside, and I felt sadder still. One of the monochrome stars on the wall I have not yet mentioned here is Leonard Cohen. I thought of some lines from one of his songs:

> Your beauty lost to you yourself
> Just as it was lost to them.

From inside or outside, will that beautiful world ever be known?

It seems to me that as long as there is an inside and an outside, it will not.

I have wondered in a vague and wistful way whether there might be a key to this in the figure of A., who appears to be neither French nor American, but, since the dividing line disappeared for him a while ago, is perhaps both.

"The fundamental delusion of humanity is to suppose that I am here and you are out there."

24th May

絶

學

無

憂

With or without hope, life goes on. Hope is, in a sense, academic.

Returning to England I have faced the usual struggles and dilemmas. My finances are such that I dare not think about them. I have, anyway, increased my work hours. This is the best job I have ever had. I knock on doors in the housing estates of one of the London boroughs and speak to people about environmental issues, trying to encourage them to use less water and electricity, to recycle, to take a re-usable bag to the supermarket, and so on. Before Paris I was working two days a week. Now I am working three. I still have time to write, though not as much as I would really like. Also, I don't have to spend my day in an office in front of a computer screen. I walk around in the fresh—or relatively fresh—air. I am not creating wealth for some businessman somewhere—the quintessence of left-brained Western materialism—but doing something I more-or-less believe in. I like the people I work with. I had no difficulties getting time off to go to Paris. The only problem is, although I am trying to encourage people to inch towards sustainable living, my own life is financially unsustainable, since the pay is simply inadequate. I suppose the assumption is that we will be taking other work to supply the rest of the money we need. My 'other work' is writing, which supplies almost no money at all.

When we had our training and were given our contracts, we were told that, naturally, we should look presentable while we are working, since we are dealing directly with the public. We were also given uniforms, with the bright yellow reflector jackets worn by traffic policemen, dustmen and so on.

On days when I work, I try to choose a pair of socks in which the holes are not showing. If there are holes where the toes are, or at the heels, it does not matter, but holes at ankle-height or above may give the wrong impression. Perhaps I should also get my hair cut soon.

Some of the estates where we are sent to do our door-knocking are quite fascinating to me. I feel like I want to read about their history. I rather think, however, that they contain all that history will forget. There are some wonderfully decrepit buildings, their architecture and general ambience conjuring up an otherworldly bleakness that few artists have ever captured. You will find something like it in the works of Thomas Ligotti and Mark Samuels. I sometimes rather despise people who treat other people's misfortune in a purely aesthetic way, but, I'm quite sincere about my fascination with the housing estates. Besides which, I don't really think people are poor unfortunates simply because they are living there. It's not so simple and I am not—I hope—so condescending. The fact is, I never know who will answer the door when I knock. This, too, is fascinating. Two entirely different worlds can co-exist in close proximity. One door opens on one world. The next door opens on a different world.

Just the other day we visited an estate whose name conjured up to me a workhouse with which I am familiar from historical reading, which became infamous as a place where some of the poor had resorted to cannibalism in their dire hunger. And on this estate, one of the blocks of flats bore a name uncannily close to 'Dracula House'. The team leader was frightened away from a flat on the ground floor when the resident let out a rather menacing dog of the pitbull variety. One of the lifts had its doors permanently open, and had not quite descended level with the floor. We got in the other lift, which creaked and squeaked very slowly upwards. At one point there was a jolt, and for a few terrible moments we thought the lift was stuck. However, we finally made it to the top floor and stepped out in collective relief. I looked about admiringly at the area in front of the lift. The ceiling was high. The walls were a patchwork of metal plates and other materials, as if the whole thing were an entirely makeshift construction. Doors led to the landings where the flats were. These doors were meant to be locked, but the trouble of gaining access was saved for us by the fact that the doors had been kicked in or their locks otherwise broken. Looking from the landings, like extended concrete balconies, the entire bulk of the building spread before and below me like a massive multi-storey car park. I was particularly fascinated by the concrete half-cylinders that protruded from the walls at regular intervals. I later discovered that these enclosed the dark, pigeon-haunted stairwells of what seemed to be mezzanine flats. Walking along these concrete balconies, I encounter all kinds of aromas. There are smells of cooking, and the oddly dusty smell of soap suds.

Some landings are caked in the most glorious dust and grime, suggesting an accumulation of so many years that it has, in its state of neglect, being entirely that which is most ignored in the world, achieved a half-haunting, half-liberating timelessness. I wonder what a microscope would reveal in this filth. I almost feel, looking at it, that to fall down here would result in a contamination that could never be eradicated. Just yesterday, on the estate we visited, we were looking for access to a block that proved to be a real treasure house of grime. We saw an open doorway, which I at first mistook for a toilet. Actually it led to the lifts and the stairwell, but my impression was not entirely mistaken. After we had finished knocking the doors on the top floor, we descended by the stairs to find them not only black with filth, but also foul with the smell of urine. On one landing I detected a different note in the foulness, and looking, found what I had expected. There were what appeared to be human faeces. They did not seem to be fresh, but were also half-covered with the black grime that was everywhere else, and half-smeared across the floor.

There is an end-of-the-world feel to such places. This atmosphere works on me in some obscure way to make me feel somehow a little freer. On the top floor of this building, for instance, was what I assumed to be one of the chutes often found in these places for the disposal of waste, around the sturdy metal doors of which there sometimes buzz flies, and from which, on hot afternoons, there emanate all kinds of lethal stenches. This particular specimen caught my imagination, and I wanted to take a photograph of it. It became, in my eyes, something like the furnace of a boiler room. The atmosphere I am trying to describe is, I decided, like that of some abandoned railway station at the end of time. Whether or not that makes sense, that is the phrase that occurs to me. I also said that this grime achieves timelessness, and there is something incredibly blissful and piquant in treading this grimy timelessness while the sun is shining and summer breezes — and it might as well be summer, whatever the calendar says — sigh in from some blue nowhere. But is this feeling truly timeless? Yes and no. If I analyse it, it does not take me long to conclude that somehow this atmosphere takes me back to the 1970s, the decade of my birth. The 70s are home to me, and home is timelessness. Well, I deal with this subject in *Domesday Afternoon*. And the 70s are, of course, the starting point for the particular kind of doomy, low-budget television sci-fi that perhaps first made me gasp and sigh inwardly with rapture at the thought of the end of the world. The end of the world in a silent patch of sooty, greasy filth on the floor of a broken-paned, abandoned railway station. In the 1970s. It's a circle. The decade in which I was born is also the decade which, by dint of its special ambience, must contain the end of time. I return home to die, and where beginning and end meet I find timelessness.

25th May

I have said that I never know who will answer the door when I knock, but two examples in particular stick in my mind. The first was in the 'Dracula House' block of flats. It was rather a gloomy concrete landing-cum-balcony, made to feel a little like a bunker by the two concrete stairwells leading up to the mezzanine flats. As usual, most of the flats were empty, since it was mid-day, or the occupants were not responding. This large-scale sense of absence is also pleasing to me, being somehow half-desolate, half-peaceful. I moved on to the next door, by now practised in not thinking about who would answer. At first there was silence, but then I heard sounds from within. Finally, the door swung open. I seemed to be peering down into some sort of barren cell. There was grey gloom and emptiness and a shaft of bleak daylight. I saw no decoration and no furniture except for a chair on which there flicked the page of an old newspaper, such as might be used to put on the floor when painting a room. I also noticed some empty or open cans of drink. Standing before me in unkempt clothes and a baseball hat was a figure who looked like some dusty emanation of the stirring wind within this cell. His skin was grey, and his mouth smudged with drool. There was something indescribable about his bearing that startled me. I may talk about giving up hope, I thought, but here is someone for whom the notion of hope has long been irrecoverable and immaterial. Here is living death, a genuine zombie, walking the Earth. Taken aback as I was, mundane instincts took hold and I began my bathetic spiel about making small differences in one's lifestyle for the sake of the environment. I had got only part way through when the man gave a dead, dry rattle in his throat, like some dusty wind escaping from a tomb, and reached out his right hand to take the 'pledge card' I held, on which were listed the various suggestions for changes to be made.

"Okay," I said, understanding by this that perhaps the man had heard enough. He took the card, and then began to raise his left arm. I am not sure what I was thinking. I only felt in some wordless way that communication was taking place between us. I even felt that I understood this communication somehow, though I cannot translate it into language. The arm rose, gesturing towards some meaning emerging between us that we both, apparently, knew. And then I saw that the end of the sleeve was limp, and inside the shirt cuff was no hand, but only shadow and absence. And then the door closed.

The second example is from the block of flats with the foul-smelling stairway. It was on the top floor. The doors here were mainly black, set into a black wall, the thickness of the dust revealed here and there by finger marks and so on. I knocked on one of the doors, and, after a while, it was opened, only for me to see no one there. I heard a sound, and there, holding the door open, was a small boy of about two or three years. Inside I saw stairs and darkness. The boy was brown-skinned, with bright, somehow plaintive eyes. I asked him if his mother or father were at home. He made the same noise he had before. It sounded to me a little like a slurred version of the Japanese 'hai', but this boy was not Japanese, and I supposed this was my imagination. Very often I am greeted by people who do not speak English, or sometimes who explain lucidly and articulately that they cannot speak English. ("I'm very sorry. I have trouble understanding English. Is it important? Maybe you could come back at a later time.") I wondered if this boy's family could speak English. Perhaps he was too young to speak any language at all. He simply stood there, holding the door open, and making the same sound to everything I said. I saw that it was no good persisting and said goodbye, telling the boy to close the door. I walked on and still he held the door open and made his little sound. I went back to him. I wondered why he had come to the door. He looked lost. Had he seen his parents answer the door and thought somehow that if he only made the same actions he could face whatever unknown thing from the great unknown world out there came knocking? In fact, he reminded me a little of the man from Dracula House. Neither had seemed to have words with which to communicate, but only inchoate sound.

I told him to close the door and go back inside, motioning with my hand in the hope of conveying my meaning, but he only stared up at me and made that sound again, like some inarticulate question. Once more I gave up and walked away. After a while, the door closed.

There are many different worlds behind these doors, and it seems incredible that there is enough of a world beyond these worlds to sustain them all, or even to have sustained them all so far, since it now seems that, after all, the world has become overburdened with worlds. When I knock on their doors, I find that some of these smaller worlds care about the big world. Although this is precisely what I am trying to encourage in my job, sometimes it seems mysterious to me that they should care at all, and I cannot quite fathom it. Does the big world care about the little worlds? Evidence would seem to suggest not. Of course, there are selfish reasons to care. The little worlds can't exist without the big world. And yet there's still some wonderful kind of mystery here that any conscience or reflection should exist to make that tiny, fragile decision to turn off the television, or buy food with less packaging.

Not all of the little worlds care, by any means, and there's a kind of mystery here, too. Whenever one of the worlds on whose door I knock tells me that he or she does not care, I immediately find it strange and alien. In simple terms it seems like a perverse unfriendliness. And yet, isn't this more in keeping with the blind, voracious will of the big world? None of these worlds asked to be born. Sometimes I feel I cannot blame them if they think the big world can go to hell, where they think they will be waiting for it, anyway. In such cases we are trained not to argue. We are to smile and be polite, thank the little worlds for their time, and move on. It is not obligatory to care. Every world is free not to care, and we do not, cannot force them. And the big world is free to starve us, flood us, visit plagues and tornadoes upon us. This freedom is like the freedom to bring into the world those who never asked to be born. All worlds, little and big, are free, and so nothing can be helped at all. We try to tame worlds; they remain wild, out of control.

I spoke to S. about such things on the telephone yesterday. We had a long and quite animated conversation. At one point I said that, the issue that no one really wants to confront when discussing the environment is the fundamental problem of overpopulation. When S. asked me what could be done about such a thing, I suggested sterilisation. She did not seem keen on the idea, and, of course, no one is. The right of people to bring into the world those who never asked to be born remains inviolate. That is the fundamental, blind, voracious, uncaring freedom of the big world. To care, paradoxically, means that you become uncaring. ("They want children? Tough luck!") I knew I was on dangerous ground. "But," I said, "the population *will* be controlled, if not by prevention, then by cure. If we don't control the population ourselves then it will be controlled by floods, famine, wars over dwindling resources, and so on."

She acknowledged the dilemma. If it is a dilemma rather than a mere state of affairs. Our desire to tame life, to control nature, has got out of control. Our population is running wild. We have no desire to control the overpopulation that is the result of our control. But the wildness of our controlling will be tamed and controlled by the wildness of nature. Her wildness will control ours. Or rather, our wildness will control itself, since our wildness is, in the end, hers. There is nothing to be done about it.

"It's this dilemma," I said, "that tends to make me think existence is inherently evil."

To exist is to be a part of the blind, voracious fight for survival. Virtue, therefore, so it seems, tends towards non-existence in direct proportion to its purity.

But if everything is evil, how can there be any judgement?

What if I demanded that we should stop bringing into the world those who have never asked to be born? What evil is avoided thereby? The evil of suffering, but whose? For certain I can only say the evil of my own conceptual suffering at the thought of all these people who have never asked to be born nonetheless being flung out into the unbearable and uncaring freedom of the big world, which renders all things helpless. It is the fact that nothing matters that is the source of this great evil—the big world not caring about the little worlds—but if nothing matters then it makes no difference whether people go on being born or not. All that then concerns me is my own suffering in the face of all this.

We were talking back and forth about the dilemma of human existence, and the looming problems of climate change. If we're not going to control the population, I said, then the only choice we had was to utterly demolish the edifice of capitalism and replace it with something else, but I did not see how this was possible when our huge cities, which do nothing but consume resources, demand capitalism for their very existence, or at least the consumption of capitalism. Cities, it seems, are nothing but huge parasites of human vanity draining and despising the countryside.

S. suggested that maybe we could use horses instead of cars. I thought it a nice, picturesque idea, but wondered if it would really make any difference. It kept coming back to me that there are simply too many people, whatever rearranging of our materialist furniture we do to try and accommodate them all.

It was one of those conversations in which your mind makes so many connections, and so many things occur to you, that most of them have to go unsaid.

I was in the back yard now, talking on the portable handset. As I was doing so, I was looking down at the paving stones of the yard, fascinated by the weeds that were growing up between the cracks. They seemed to me extraordinarily beautiful. I thought to myself that, in the context of this conversation, S. might very much appreciate a quote from the song 'Stretch Out and Wait':

> Amid concrete and clay
> And general decay
> Nature must still find a way.

It has always been one of my favourite quotes from The Smiths. This, however, was one of those things that remained unsaid.

Looking at the weeds, which seemed to resemble something like a miniaturised nasturtium, or a kind of clover, a strange sensation flooded over me, even as we spoke. This sensation, too, and its accompanying thoughts, remained unspoken. Even writing them here I wonder if they will sound either enormously exaggerated or flat and unremarkable. I will do my best not to misrepresent them.

I felt myself to be that sprouting weed. It was as if I saw my death and my life at the same time in its little canopy of leaves. The leaves, being separate and ramified, were like something breaking up. I saw myself as a decaying body, crumbling and collapsing, and from the collapse there came an explosion of life in this slow-to-stillness firework of stem and leaves. It was not, as I experienced it, a lonely sensation. It was not some inadequate sop to console me in my human mortality. It was very simple. I saw the weed. I saw my death. I saw my life. It was good.

It was after this that I said, at what seemed an appropriate point in the conversation:

"But, I've come to think, to feel, that really nothing matters at all. Really. Nothing matters at all. It's just very difficult to be human."

And why is it difficult to be human? Because—it's very simple—we think our little worlds are separate from the big world. We have the sensation—right or wrong or neither or both—that we are agonising over making the right decisions, that we are responsible for things, that we think and act independently. We simply have to suffer this anomalous sensation.

S. agreed that, of course, ultimately, nothing did matter, but felt that in human life, for her, what was important was to take care of those close to you, to make their lives and your own life better where possible, to create pockets of beauty, for instance with art, and so on.

It seemed we had come full circle to the question of caring or not caring. To care or not to care. And all the small, fragile decisions that spring from these two states.

And humans who have never asked to be born will go on bringing more humans who never asked to be born into the world, as if there's really no helping it at all. And these humans, lost in the wild, uncaring freedom of the big world, will puzzle over whether to care or not to care, as if the choice were theirs to make and as if it made a difference. And . . . perhaps it even does.

26th May

I am ignorant, and all I have written, I imagine, is evidence of this. Perhaps that's one reason I prefer fiction to philosophy, and the pursuit of beauty to the promotion of politics. The only ability in which I have had a scrap of confidence, though only a scrap, is my ability to imagine, and so fiction seems all that I am truly qualified for. Even in that, it's best if it's fiction of a fantastic or dreamy cast. Artistically or otherwise, I feel that the only achievement for which nature has in some way equipped me is beauty, and that even if I fulfil such a potential, it must only be in the lowliest and most fleeting of ways.

In Paris I had occasion to feel this ignorance of mine quite keenly and with a greater frequency than I do at home in England. I am not sure if this is something to do with France, or something to do with S., or both. I suspect that there is less shame in being intelligent and cultured in France than there is in Britain. While I was there we came across an old chestnut I've encountered before, this time in an interview with a British writer in a French arts magazine. The writer trotted out the chestnut (or whatever you do with chestnuts), as follows: "In France, all writers are important. In America, only successful writers are important. And in England, if you say you're a writer, they say, 'So what?'"

The version I knew ends slightly differently, thus:

"In England no writers are important. And in Australia you have to explain what a writer is."

In any case, it seems, in all its bitterness, true to me, about England, if nothing else.

S. asked me at one point what it's like to have a queen, and I hardly knew how to answer this, but I wonder if, somewhere, at some culturally subconscious level, the presence of 'Her Majesty' does not perpetuate the disgusting class consciousness that makes it somehow shameful for a working-class person to read books or use words of more than two syllables. Perhaps without her the arts would suddenly seem more egalitarian.

Whatever the case might be in terms of French and English culture, it is certainly true that at an individual level I am more ignorant, or less cultured, than S. This seems to me entirely obvious, and yet when I mention this she dismisses the idea that she is, for instance, well read, with a modesty in which there is not a shadow of falseness. Can she really take her knowledge, education and so on so much for granted?

On the very first day I arrived in Paris, when we got to S.'s room, I found myself beginning an impassioned (or my version of impassioned) speech about education, and how I was never given any in England, and am only now, halfway through my life, in my blind, groping way, beginning to discover what is out there to be known and considered. It seems as if all that was most important—all aspects of history, philosophy, art, literature, religion and so on most likely to give a sense of context to the human situation by which we might orientate ourselves—was maliciously hidden from us, and all that was most trivial—the monkey tricks best calculated to please our future paymasters—forced upon us before we had time to wonder who we were and what was happening.

S. informed me that the situation was the same in France, that that was precisely why she had taken herself out of school—to give herself a decent education. Apparently it has worked, and I can't think of a better indictment at the moment of institutional education.

When S. came to ask me, at the end of my visit, how my experience had been, one thing I mentioned was the fact that I had felt ignorant on a number of occasions.

27th May

She seemed somewhat dismayed to hear this, as if she had somehow been remiss. Actually, though, I think it is a good thing to be humbled. I feel better for it.

Recently I have been especially fascinated by the twentieth chapter of the *Tao Te Ching*. I read this to S. over the phone one day, before my visit, and she was suitably impressed. She bought a copy soon thereafter. I took my writing brushes to Paris with me, as well as the original text of the *Tao Te Ching*, and offered to write out some of it for her in Chinese if she wished. She chose the twentieth chapter.

Considering how much I felt the need to improve my own education while in Paris, I found the first line of the twentieth chapter strikingly ironic. This line, in the pithy, elemental style of classical Chinese, consists of only four ideograms: 絕 學 無 憂. (*Jue xue wu you.*) These four characters (Chinese, or Mandarin, at least, seems to abound in maxims and aphorisms of fours characters) are usually translated as something like, "Abandon learning and end your cares." (Stop study, no grief.) Considering the amount of worry it costs me when I think of all the catching up I have to do, this seems to make perfect sense. As I have remarked before, actually, you can never catch up. So why not give up?

And yet, I feel education to be important. Part of the irony I mentioned consists in the fact that it has taken me a fair amount of learning to be able to write in Chinese the characters of an ancient text advocating the abandonment of learning. And, of course, whoever wrote the text in the first place—Lao Tze, apparently—must have had a considerable amount of learning under his belt, since I imagine literacy must have been very rare two and a half thousand years ago.

Perhaps I'm only interpreting the text to suit my own inclinations, but it seems to me that this line is not to be taken literally as an injunction to end anything resembling study immediately. I'm very much an amateur here, but having scrutinized the original text I notice many ideograms are not used in their modern meaning, and I wonder if '*xue*' ('study') here might be one of them. Even if the word was generally used at the time in a way analogous to its modern application, I have a certain understanding of the text as a whole that leads me to think a literal interpretation would be foolish.

But if learning does not mean learning, then what does it mean? Well, I'm tempted to think that it refers to a specific attitude that is usually part of learning. It is the effort, through learning, to become learnéd.

There is a sense in which intellectual striving assumes some goal of perfection, some ultimate accomplishment, but what is it? When will you finally be learnéd? When will you solve all your problems through study? Or the world's problems? Clearly the state of finally being learnéd can never be achieved, and if it were, would still solve nothing. You can never catch up. In other words, it is this effort to catch up with something that does not even exist which should be abandoned, not necessarily learning itself, though I suppose it might be said that the line in question also refers to the way in which rational thought and its tendency to categorise creates only an expanding confusion that must be supported by expanding intellectualization in a vicious spiral that is the cause of much or all unhappiness.

For the moment I'm sticking with my interpretation — abandon the effort to catch up. *Wei wu wei*. Do without doing.

This seems to me to explain why academic study of literature often renders literature somehow impotent and meaningless. Try to make something useful, and it becomes useless. It becomes a mere tool for an end that never really arrives. Those who follow too closely this particular path of education and career, themselves become tools, part of a useful machine that is ultimately the most useless thing of all.

The more useless something is, however, the more useful it becomes, since it makes no demands. Like a friend, it simply lives and allows you simply to live. And so Nagai Kafū's dilettante fictions, which serve no purpose whatsoever, but are like beautiful sighs, have saved my life.

I wonder if it is, after all, possible to teach these, the most important aspects of being human, or whether anything that is taught does not automatically become academic.

My dictionary gives 'academic' as "abstract, un-practical, theoretical, cold, merely logical". People often say, "Well, that's an academic question." They mean it's not important. It makes no difference. I suppose I approve of learning in so far as it starts out as useless—learning for learning's sake. If it is utilitarian in attitude then it becomes 'academic', as this explanation is in danger of being.

I used the word 'academic' earlier in this notebook. I said that hope is academic. Maybe the academic is also a kind of hope. "Abandon hope, and end your cares."

I have tried to abandon hope, but so far it has not worked. I have given up trying to give up. No, that's not true. I continue to try, and therefore continue to fail. I think about this a great deal in relation to my writing. I want to succeed. My writing is therefore contaminated by ambition. It has occurred to me that the very act of writing is hopelessly hopeful and ambitious and that I should give the activity up. And what happens when we give up? Presumably that's something we have to find out after we give up. I have a notion that after I give up writing that what I will do is write, but that I will do it better.

That is speculation. I have not been able to give up anything, and as a result I despair and wonder what I am living for. I will never catch up.

After coming back from Paris, something made me pick up the translation of Nagai Kafū's *Okamezasa*

(*Dwarf Bamboo*) that I started some years ago. I decided to start working on it again. Re-reading it had brought back to me with especial freshness that sense of exquisite uselessness that is the reason I love Kafū. This translation is not my own writing, as such. It will take a long time to finish, and the end is so far off I cannot see it. At best, it will earn me a pittance, or it may not be published at all, or only published by someone unwilling to pay. No one is waiting for me to finish this. And yet, the mere fact that this useless thing exists is a source of such satisfaction to me that I simply cannot explain it, and the fact I cannot explain it is part of the satisfaction. It is like the most elegant and glorious two-fingered salute to the entire rest of the useful world out there that could possibly exist. This is what I have decided to do, because I could, it seems to say.

I re-read the author's foreword, in which he explains the reason for choosing the title, *Dwarf Bamboo*:

> Bamboo is, as a rule, an emblem of elegance. However, dwarf bamboo, part of the same bamboo family, is somewhat different. This people tread on, this they relieve themselves on. It grows thick as weeds always at the edges of fields and the sides of paths. When some perverse old codger like myself capriciously decides, in mock-refinement, to cultivate this plant, the poor gardener is quite bewildered by his request to plant it in his garden. Look and you will see in this the heart of my foolish work.

If there is too much of hope in my own writing to give me a reason to live, then perhaps, for now, *Dwarf Bamboo* can be my reason.

29th May

There was a curious, personal postscript for me to the Sargent exhibition we attended in Paris. This postscript took the form of a television programme broadcast about a week ago, comparing the work of Sargent and Sickhert. In fact, the title was *Sargent vs. Sickhert*. This caught my attention because, not only had I been to the Sargent exhibition, but one of my first thoughts while I was there was that Sargent's style was somewhat reminiscent of Sickhert's. Watching this television programme I began to think that, after all, they were not so similar, which makes it all the more unusual that they should be paired in this way after I had paired them in my own head. But, after all, maybe it was merely because they were contemporaries, or *contrasting* contemporaries.

Some of what I had instinctively felt about Sargent from his paintings was confirmed by the programme. Sickhert liked the fleapit sleaze of the music hall. Sargent preferred to remain safe in the lofty comfort of a box at the opera house.

Needless to say (?), long before the programme had reached its conclusion, I felt myself leaning emphatically towards Sickhert.

When the conclusion did come it echoed what I had been consciously thinking throughout, but also dug up some considerations in me that had been—at least during my viewing of the programme—buried.

The critic who was presenting summed up the comparisons made so far. If you want the nineteenth century, he said, Sargent's your man. His capturing of the age on canvas was immaculate. Sickhert, however, had more than the nineteenth century. Preoccupied by the tawdry celebrities of music hall, by prostitution, murder, isolation, alienation and urban anxiety, his works were like an artistic matrix in which the twentieth century was gestating. I understood this. I particularly connected with the painting, 'The Camden Town Murder', which shows a male figure, head bowed, sitting upon the edge of a bed in some insalubrious flat with a naked woman sprawled behind him. He seems to be preoccupied with his hands. Perhaps he is wringing them. They are red, as with blood, though this may be a trick of the light. The woman could be sleeping. Or perhaps she is lifeless.

There is, anyway, a brooding aura about the painting—of what? It is hard to say. Remorse? Loneliness? Or is it that "nameless dread" that is so recurrent in *American Psycho* and seems to form the very heart of the modern age? This foreshadowing of the modern age, the presenter concluded, certainly made Sickhert the better painter. But he wondered, in a way that at first seemed flippant and nonsensical, whether that was really a good thing.

We have arrived at an age, it seems, when reasons *not* to kill yourself are harder and harder to come by. I feel that we, and particularly I, have somehow 'ended up' here—'ended up' is certainly the phrase. Recently I received an e-mail from Thomas Ligotti Online telling me that Ligotti's latest work, *The Conspiracy Against the Human Race*, a long philosophical treatise on why human life is inexcusably horrible, was available for free download for a limited period. Naturally, I leapt at the chance to read it.

Having read a number of portions of the text in a kind of trance of will-crushing dread, I find that it deals with many of the themes that have occupied me in this notebook, although the conclusions drawn—not that I have read the final conclusion, which Ligotti tells us at the beginning is, anyway, foregone—are slightly at variance with my own.

Inasmuch as this is what universal consciousness has washed up on the shore of my consciousness, it is, however, mine. I feel that it is what we have all come to, where we have all 'ended up'.

The treatise runs to upwards of a hundred pages. I will attempt a digest of what I have read here.

For Ligotti, consciousness, and specifically human consciousness, is an aberration in creation, and an obscenity. We are the only animals who are aware that we are alive and that we will die. As he has stated elsewhere, "It's a damn shame that intelligent life ever evolved in the first place." It is imperative for human beings, against all evidence and against all odds, to pretend that there is some meaning to this state of affairs—the emergence of their aberrant consciousness and the animal mortality of which it makes them aware—if they wish to survive. However, survival only means further suffering, which is dealt with by further lies about there being some meaning to life.

Eventually the entire human race will end, anyway, and eternity will continue ever away from the blip of our existence, so any kind of meaning or immortality stops there. Would it not be better, at least, to reduce the needless suffering by ceasing to procreate?

This, to me, is the only logical and viable *atheist* position. It is atheism's logical conclusion. I admire Ligotti's thoroughness in taking such a position and fleshing it out. As far as I have read it, the essay seems to leave us with three options from which to choose:

a) lies
b) insanity
c) voluntary extinction

There is some overlap between a and b, if they are not entirely identical. Although they might facilitate our further survival, neither of them makes us proof against pain, and, of course, neither of them will ever bring us final satisfaction.

The text of the essay is impeccably well written. This is not a question of mere style. Every word seems to fall with due gravitas into its natural place, like water finding its level, giving the impression of something, on its own terms, indisputable. The author has carried this work with him for a long time. This is not academic. It feels like the summation of a life. I do not doubt that this is a serious and considerable work, though I've no idea how the academic cliques might receive it. I am not an academic. I am, however, a bit of a flibbertigibbet. Anything I write in a notebook like this is bound to be a little flighty and flimsy and I do not hope to give the work the response it deserves. I only think that it is most definitely THERE, and cannot be ignored.

There is nothing I can put into words of which I am certain, and this effectively means that I am not an atheist, if for no other reason than that atheism is just another word. When you are not an atheist, the three options previously mentioned begin to look different and change. In particular, the first option may be replaced by others. Some may even be creative enough to come up with more than three options. In my own case, I have never been entirely able to persuade myself that reasons for living are either lies or truth. It seems to me that there may indeed be a meaning to existence. Why? Why not? I mean, why shouldn't there be? Oh, nothing to do with words, of course. I noticed an interesting phrase in Ligotti's essay, in quotation marks. Even most intellectual writers, he says, fall short of complete nihilism and back on "what the heart knows". I can't say I've noticed a great deal of this among intellectuals myself, but it's certainly something that is true of me. At least, the phrase means something to me, however it was intended.

Anyway, there may be a meaning to life, and if so, it is my task as a writer to discover it. Not that I can express it directly. It would have to exist between the lines. I'm entirely aware of how trite and naive that sounds, but there it is. I won't dress it up or down.

As I said, I am certain of nothing I can put into words, but for me the dilemma of existence goes something like this: If evil exists in the world, and it certainly does, then the entire universe must be evil, because a benevolent universe could not possibly support evil. Therefore the universe, if it falls below perfection at any point, and it has, must be evil. So, let's say the universe is evil. In that case, how is it that I am able to experience anything as good at all—the beautiful things I see, the people who seem always to have had a place in my heart. Where do these things come from in a universe that is entirely evil? You can't make a silk purse out of a sow's ear, as they say, and however many times you add evil to evil, it still equals evil. Good cannot spring up *ex nihilo*, and therefore can only come from a universe that is entirely good (one that is only slightly good is, as we have seen, already entirely evil). Therefore the universe is entirely good. But if so, where does evil come from? Etcetera.

You could say, theologically, or philosophically speaking, that I swing both ways. It has really cost me more than I can ever explain, and continues to do so.

For me, anyway, the jury is still out. Until a verdict is returned, a unanimous verdict, you might say, I believe it is best to err on the side of caution and refrain from procreation.

Ironically, if all were to adopt such a policy, it would probably preclude any verdict ever being returned, anyway.

Moreover, I have neither the power nor the inclination to enforce such a policy beyond my own life.

When it comes down to it, the whole thing is absurd.

If it's a problem then it's my problem. And if it's only my problem, it really doesn't make any difference at all. Nothing matters.

We are all lost in nothing-matters.

And instead of words there comes the thought of . . .

. . . through the round window . . .

It's all a dream.

It's all a dream.

I hear a voice calling my name, feel a hand on my chest.

Quentin . . . waiting . . . so long . . .

. . . 1972 . . .

Wake up, butterfly.

I close my eyes and I see . . .

I see a butterfly, fluttering from flower to flower.

You are sleeping. You do not want to believe.

There's light falling all warm and yellow from the barn door. People are dancing inside. The music is . . . I am standing outside, where it seems I always was, in the dark and the cold.

Remember me!

Remember me!

Missing . . . me . . . missing . . .

. . . Japanese knotweed . . .

I look back to my childhood and forward to my death.

There is a light . . .

Meet me.

. . . 722 Love Avenue . . .

I am waiting.

. . . I am in love . . . in love with everything . . .

For so long.

. . . in Montauk . . . the light . . .

In my chest.

My name.

You know me already.

I always said that somehow the aim of my name was true, and I was given my true, secret name by accident, to wear on the outside, where it hurts. And that's why you can see the head of a little boy when you write a capital Q, and the tail in the middle is the little curl across his forehead, the crisp little lick of hair.

I once wrote the words to a song called 'Missing'. It began, "I want to go missing with you/I believe, yes, I believe/That everything is true."

I've always been afraid that what I am made of is lies, and that what the lies make me is insane.

. . . I know it . . . beneath the falls . . .

There. Where? There.

The City of Aira . . .

I can still see it now. Also known as Hôrai, where the fairies drink from tiny cups.

The deadly winds from the West . . .

. . . a light . . .

Life is but a dream.

. . . J. repeats the word "*autotrophe*" at the dinner table and laughs for reasons unknown to the rest of us . . .

Life is butterfly dream.

31st May

This morning a letter arrived from France. Inside the envelope, in a bag, separate to the letter, was the post-card I had requested, in the 'China, Shanghai' series.

There were a number of things for which we had not had time on that last day. I had meant to remind

S. of one of them, but apparently she remembered, anyway. When we were in the last tea shop, where I had read from *The Book of Tea* and cried, I had taken photographs of our tea and cakes. S. remarked on this habit I have of photographing what I am about to eat. I wondered if she found it silly or amusing, but she replied that it was not at all silly, and, in fact, that it reminded her of passages in the works of Marcel Proust and Denton Welch about cakes. She said she would read me the Denton Welch passage on the train to the station, but as it turned out we were too hurried and flustered for that, and the projected scene never took place. However, without my prompting, S. had transcribed the passage in the letter to me.

In the passage, the protagonist, Orvil, goes to a restaurant on his own and orders four different cakes. The passage ends thus:

> He fixed his gaze on the distance until the waiter left him; then he bowed his head, opened the book, and began to eat.

The red paper bag containing the postcard (incidentally, red envelopes, or *'hong bao'*, are used with traditional New Year gifts in China, as red is an auspicious colour) allowed me to hesitate and anticipate before I drew the postcard out and discovered which S. had chosen.

What was I expecting? I hardly knew, but here it was, hardened into fact. Yes, there was the same, faded, dreamy, pastel ambience, the predominant colours pink and yellow. Just today I was reading about Chinese pink and yellow in Denton Welch's *Maiden*

Voyage. A character called Mr. Butler complains of a Chinese cup he is using, "Why will the Chinese, in spite of all their refinement, insist on putting yellow next to pink? Just look at these blowsy great peonies sprawling on the jaundiced sides of my cup."

Denton's response is as follows:

> I looked, and thought the arrangement
> very gay and pretty.

I agree with Denton on this one.

After a moment—a very short moment—the general pastel pink-and-yellow ambience shrank into a specific image, with the hard and shrunken look of certain ivory antiques.

Then I began to take in the details. I had seen this image in the shop, but I scrutinized it afresh.

The central picture, framed by a pattern incorporating the character *'fu'* or 'luck' (I have always interpreted this as a kind of divine luck), by the name in Chinese of a tobacco company at the top, and by smaller pictures of cigarettes in tins and boxes at the bottom, is of two young women at a round table in front of a window, in what I suppose to be a drawing room. The two women, whose faces I want to call 'peach-like', seem to bear a family resemblance, and could be sisters. One is sitting at the table and one standing behind, or next to her. Both have tiny, delicately painted red lips. The standing figure wears a Chinese silk dress with a predominantly black-and-yellow pattern. Hanging from her neck is a string of pearls, and perhaps hanging from these, or fastened to her dress, facing downwards, are two roses, one

116

large, one small. Her black hair is smooth and disciplined. It seems to have a right-hand side-parting. Her hairline arches from her ears, coming to a tufty, kiss-curl point in the middle of her forehead. At the level of her earlobes, pierced with pearl earrings, her hair bunches into curls. Pencil-line eyebrows float over eyes both penetrating and dreamy. Her left hand reaches towards the table, where it grasps a black, box-like object, perhaps a book, as if about to pick it up and open it.

The seated figure wears a reddish dress. She shares with her sister—apart from the red lips—the thin, floating eyebrows, the dreamy, penetrating eyes, the smooth, disciplined hair, and the pearl earrings. Her hair is styled slightly differently, however. She has a centre parting, and, instead of a little tuft, she has what the Americans refer to as 'bangs'. Her chin is resting on the back of her left hand. The elbow of her right arm rests on the pages of an open book. The book appears to be blank. Next to the book is a black, three-legged vase, in which there is a blossoming spray from a tree. The blossoms are pink, and could be peach. The pistils at their centre are yellow. After all, it seems even nature approves this colour scheme. The seated sister holds one of the blossoming twigs in her right hand, which is inclined towards her left shoulder, almost as if this were some obscure sort of peach-blossom salute. Behind her head, the lower portion of the window is latticed, in that peculiar Chinese style, resembling somewhat the pattern forming the picture's border. I have a feeling, perhaps mistaken, that this lattice pattern is some kind of extrapolation of the character '*fu*', or the double '*xi*', which is also auspicious.

Through the window is a slightly blurred and blotted landscape of different greens, predominantly dark, suggesting fields and buildings and, further in the distance, wooded hills. From the slope of one of the hills, something rises up vertically, like a tower.

Returning to the foreground I discover something I missed at first. The right hand of the standing figure seems to be resting on her sister's shoulder, and the hand that seemed before to be supporting the seated figure's chin, is perhaps reaching quietly across to touch it. Now that I think about it, there is something slightly different in the expressions of these two figures. One—the standing sister—seems almost to be leaning forward, as if about to say something to the unknown person outside of the patterned frame. The other, her eyes every bit as penetrating, seems as if leaning back. She will not speak at all.

※

On the train, after leaving Shakespeare and Co., I examined my purchases. S. took the Baudelaire volume and searched out something in it. She handed it back to me, telling me to read the one she had chosen. The English title was, 'The Invitation to the Voyage'.

After reading it, I said that I felt inadequate.

"But why?" asked S.

"Well, I just feel like, here was someone who lived more, felt more, thought more, experienced more and knew more than I could ever hope to, and expressed it all much better than I could, too."

Perhaps it's appropriate that I should finish now with some extracts from that piece:

Tu connais cette maladie fiévreuse qui s'em-
pare de nous dans les froides misères, cette
nostalgie du pays qu'on ignore, cette angoisse
de la curiosité? Il est une contrée qui te res-
semble, où tout est beau, riche, tranquille et
honnête, où la fantaise a bâti et décoré une
Chine occidentale, où la vie est douce a respi-
rer, où le bonheur est marié au silence. C'est
là qu'il faut aller vivre, c'est là qu'il faut aller
mourir!

. . . Des rêves! toujours des rêves! et plus
l'âme est ambitieuse et délicate, plus les rêves
l'éloignent du possible. Chaque homme porter
en lui sa dose d'opium naturel, incessament
sécrétée et renouvelée, et, de la naissance a la
mort, combine comptons-nous d'heures rem-
plies par la jouissance positive, par l'action
réussie et décidée? Vivrons-nous jamais,
passerons-nous jamais dans ce tableau qu'a
peint mon esprit, ce tableau qui te ressemble?

Fin.

Author's Afterword

5th *March, 2017, Bexleyheath*

The preceding pages are a diary I kept, with publication in mind, for about one month in 2007, almost ten years ago at the time I write these words. Reading back over it now, I find myself confronted by questions relating to time and identity.

Would the person who wrote this diary have a sense of satisfaction if he had known at the time that, ten years hence, what he wrote would be published? The fact is, he did not know and he had no such sense of satisfaction. Can I, then, be satisfied on his behalf? No—I am the future self to him unknown. What I really feel, on the threshold of publication, is something like the emotion known to a person about to make a confession that does him no credit. My confession? That I *was* this person.

This, however, brings us round in a kind of circle. I notice how different I am to the person I was, only because there is an identity that makes the comparison meaningful. Perhaps, after all, I am not as different now as I would like to think. Perhaps these two selves, separated in time, strike together a single chord and confess with one voice. Is this satisfying? Perhaps, if it is satisfying to know that we are always only beginning.

Only if there is an 'I' can I say that I have changed.

A PARTIAL LIST OF SNUGGLY BOOKS

LÉON BLOY *The Tarantulas' Parlor and Other Unkind Tales*

FÉLICIEN CHAMPSAUR *The Latin Orgy*

BRENDAN CONNELL *Metrophilias*

QUENTIN S. CRISP *September*

QUENTIN S. CRISP *October*

LADY DILKE *The Outcast Spirit and Other Stories*

BERIT ELLINGSEN *Vessel and Solsvart*

RHYS HUGHES *Cloud Farming in Wales*

JUSTIN ISIS *Divorce Procedures for the Hairdressers of a Metallic and Inconstant Goddess*

VICTOR JOLY *The Unknown Collaborator and Other Legendary Tales*

BERNARD LAZARE *The Mirror of Legends*

JEAN LORRAIN *Masks in the Tapestry*

JEAN LORRAIN *Nightmares of an Ether-Drinker*

JEAN LORRAIN *The Soul-Drinker and Other Decadent Fantasies*

CATULLE MENDÈS *Bluebirds*

DAMIAN MURPHY *Daughters of Apostasy*

KRISTINE ONG MUSLIM *Butterfly Dream*

YARROW PAISLEY *Mendicant City*

DAVID RIX *A Suite in Four Windows*

FREDERICK ROLFE *An Ossuary of the North Lagoon and Other Stories*

JASON ROLFE *An Archive of Human Nonsense*

TOADHOUSE *Gone Fishing with Samy Rosenstock*

TOADHOUSE *Living and Dying in a Mind Field*

9 781943 813407